Yankee Ghosts

Yankee Ghosts

by the author of *Where the Ghosts Are* and *Ghost Hunter*

Hans Holzer

*S*pine-tingling encounters
with the phantoms of New York and New England

YANKEE BOOKS

A division of Yankee Publishing Incorporated, Dublin, New Hampshire

Designed by Leslie Stevenson Fry

Yankee Publishing Incorporated
Dublin, New Hampshire
First Edition
Second Yankee Books printing 1986
Copyright 1966 by Hans Holzer

Library of Congress Catalog Card Number 86-80336
ISBN 0-89909-102-4

Contents

Yankee Ghost, Go Home!

When the first edition of *Yankee Ghosts* appeared some years back, and I toured the lecture and television circuit, people would ask — ghosts in New England? Why, aren't they mainly to be found in ancient English dungeons and castles of Europe? Or, at the very least, in the exotic reaches of India?

They assumed that England was so full of specters that few remained for that shining, modern, up-to-the-minute United States. There are, in fact, many more Yankee ghosts than British wraiths, as this book will show. This is as it should be, for our country is so much larger than England and the opportunities for tragic death are so much greater. Our wide-open spaces and ever-expanding big cities abound in tragedy, and what we lack in history and age, we make up in tempo of living.

Once my audiences realized that ghosts were very much at home in the U.S., they began to remember this story or that one . . . accounts of their own experiences, long forgotten, or relegated to the realm of gossip and hearsay. Before I knew it, people from the audience surged forward to the podium eager to tell me of *their* ghostly experiences, their particular favorites among the specters that walk in the night . . . and frequently in the daytime as well.

As a parapsychologist, I make a practice of sending restless ghosts to their appropriate homes beyond the veil. Sometimes they go at once. Sometimes they linger and I have to return to the haunted place once or twice to make the dismissal stick.

Ghosts are people, or parts of people, anyway, governed by emotional stimuli. It is not always easy for ghosts to tell their tales, for they are like psychotics. We are dealing with the emotional memory of a person who has died under tragic circumstances and keeps re-living those final moments over and over, unaware that death, as we know it, has occurred. Once I have established the identity and problem of the ghost, I explain the true situation to him or her, and gently but firmly send them from the house to join the loved ones who have gone before them.

My methods call for the presence of a sensitive person to pick up clairvoyantly, or through trance, tangible material about a haunted house that can then be examined for validity. I don't hold with the ghost investigator who spends a night alone in a haunted house, and then has nothing to show for his bravery but a stiff back.

The purpose of investigation is twofold: one, to establish the observed facts, and two, to make contact with the alleged ghost. The chance of seeing an apparition if you are not a sensitive is practically nil, and I do not profess to mediumship. So I usually take a good trance psychic along when I visit a haunted house.

In this book you will meet Ethel Johnson Meyers and Betty Ritter, whose credentials as mediums were well established in my earlier books. In most cases it is the late British medium Sybil Leek you will be meeting. Sybil Leek was an author in her own right and never gave private readings.

Even before we met through friends in New York, Sybil was well established in Britain. In New England, she was already known as a psychic whose predictions had often come true. Her interest in the benign aspects of ancient Druidic witchcraft had made her an authority on the subject. Less known was her great faculty as a trance medium with extremely strong control. I tested her several times before I was convinced that she was one of the truly great mediums of our time.

Betty Ritter, who worked with me as a medium specializing in precognition and a kind of traveling trance, had developed her talent for psychic photography to a remarkable degree. With only an old Kodak bellows camera and film size 116, she showed that otherwise invisible things do appear on her film beyond any possibility of fraud or accident. Entire words, letters, lines, walls of light, and crudely formed figures have all imposed themselves on her negatives. I have examined the prints and found them similar in technique to what has already been published in F. W. Warrick's *Experiments in Psychics*. I have seen ample evidence to accept the reality of psychic photography, and see great possibilities for its use in future investigations.

What is remarkable about Yankee ghosts is their human character; ghostly New Englanders have lost none of their bite and individuality from their years in the flesh, even if they are now operating from a different level of existence. A character trait particularly prevalent to the shades of New England is their tenacious clinging to earthly possessions and rights; they are house-proud people even when in the spirit realm.

Thus, dear reader, in making the accounts of my investigations into the colorful ghosts of New England available to you once again, I hope that you will also understand the ongoing need to relate to those who, for one reason or the other, are caught in the web of their own unresolved emotions at the time of physical death, who need your full understanding and, where possible, your help to move on into the wider world of spirit.

As in so many areas of human endeavor, America seems destined to be a leader in parapsychology, too. The phenomena of ghosts and hauntings, and less complicated occurrences of extrasensory perception in general, are studied more seriously in the United States than in other countries — where there is only polite interest. From the United States will come the realization that there is a non-physical factor in human personality in all of us. It will be a major accomplishment of our century when orthodox science catches up with parapsychology.

Prof. Hans Holzer, Ph.D.

"Ocean-Born" Mary

Among the ghostly legends of the United States, that of "Ocean-Born" Mary and her fascinating house at Henniker, New Hampshire, is probably one of the best known. To the average literate person who has heard about the colorful tale of Mary Wallace, or the New Englander who knows of it because he lives "Down East," it is, of course, a legend — not to be taken too seriously.

I had a vague idea of its substance when I received a note from a lady named Corinne Russell, who together with her husband, David, had bought the Henniker house and wanted me to know that it was still haunted.

That was in October of 1963. It so happens that Halloween is the traditional date on which the ghost of six-foot Mary Wallace is supposed to "return" to her house in a coach drawn by six horses. On many a Halloween, youngsters from all around Henniker have come and sat around the grounds waiting for Mary to ride in. The local press had done its share of Halloween ghost hunting, so much so that the Russells had come to fear that date as one of the major nuisance days of their year.

After all, Halloween visitors do not pay the usual fee to be shown about the house, but they do leave behind them destruction and litter at times. Needless to say, nobody has ever seen Mary ride in her coach on Halloween. Why should she when she lives there *all year round?*

To explain this last statement, I shall have to take you back to the year 1720, when a group of Scottish and Irish immigrants was approaching the New World aboard a ship called the *Wolf*, from Londonderry, Ireland. The ship's captain, Wilson, had just become the father of a daughter, who was actually born at sea. Within sight of land, the ship was boarded by pirates under the command of a buccaneer named Don Pedro. As the pirates removed all valuables from their prize, Don Pedro went below to the captain's cabin. Instead of gold, he found Mrs. Wilson and her newborn baby girl.

"What's her name?" he demanded.

Unafraid, the mother replied that the child had not yet been baptized, having been recently born.

"If you will name her after my mother, Mary," the pirate said, overcome with an emotion few pirates ever allow into their lives, "I will spare everybody aboard this ship."

Joyously, the mother made the bargain, and "Ocean-Born" Mary received her name. Don Pedro ordered his men to hand back what they had already taken from their prisoners, to set them free, and to leave the captured ship. The vicious-looking crew grumbled and withdrew to their own ship.

Minutes later, however, Don Pedro returned alone. He handed Mrs. Wilson a bundle of silk.

"For Mary's wedding gown," he said simply, and left again.

As soon as the pirate ship was out of sight, the *Wolf* continued her voyage for Boston. Thence Captain and Mrs. Wilson went on to their new home in Londonderry, New Hampshire, where they settled down, and where Mary grew up.

When she was 18, she married a man named Wallace, and over

the years they had four sons. However, shortly after the birth of the fourth son, her husband died and Mary found herself a widow.

Meanwhile, Don Pedro — allegedly an Englishman using the Spanish *nom de pirate* to disguise his noble ancestry — had kept in touch with the Wilsons. Despite the hazards of pirate life, he survived to an old age when thoughts of retirement filled his mind. Somehow he managed to acquire a land grant of 6,000 acres in what is now Henniker, New Hampshire, far away from the sea. On this land, Pedro built himself a stately house. He employed his ship's carpenters, as can be seen in the way the beams are joined. Ship's carpenters have a special way of building, and "Ocean-Born" Mary's house, as it later became known, is an example of this.

The house was barely finished when the aging pirate heard of Mary Wallace's loss of her husband, and he asked Mary and her children to come live with him. She accepted his invitation, and soon became his housekeeper.

The house was then in a rather isolated part of New England, and few callers, if any, came to interrupt the long stillness of the many cold winter nights. Mary took up painting and with her own hands created the eagle that can still be seen gracing the house.

The years went by peacefully, until one night someone attacked Don Pedro and killed him. Whether one of his men had come to challenge the pirate captain for part of the booty, or whether the reputation of a retired pirate had put ideas of treasure in the mind of some local thief, we may never know. All we know is that by the time Mary Wallace got out into the grove at the rear of the house, Don Pedro was dying with a pirate cutlass in his chest. He asked her to bury him under the hearthstone in the kitchen, which is in the rear of the house.

Mary herself inherited the house and what went with it, treasure, buried pirate, and all. She herself passed on in 1814, and ever since then the house had been changing hands.

Unfortunately, we cannot interview the earlier owners of the house, but during the 1930s, it belonged to one Louis Roy, retired and disabled and a permanent guest in what used to be his home. He sold the house to the Russells in the early sixties.

During the great hurricane of 1938, Roy claims that Mary Wallace's ghost saved his life 19 times. Trapped outside the house by falling trees, he somehow was able to get back into the house. His very psychic mother, Mrs. Roy, informed him that she had actually seen the tall, stately figure of "Ocean-Born" Mary moving behind him, as if to help him get through. In the 1950s, *Life* told this story in an illustrated article on famous ghost-haunted houses in America. Mrs. Roy claimed she had seen the ghost of Mary time and again, but since she herself passed on in 1948, I could not get any details from *her*.

Then there were two state troopers who saw the ghost, but again I could not interview them, as they, too, were also on the other side of the veil.

A number of visitors claimed to have felt "special vibrations" when touching the hearthstone, where Don Pedro allegedly was buried. There was, for instance, Mrs. James Nisula of Londonderry, who visited the house several times. She said that she and her "group" of ghost buffs had "felt the vibrations" around the kitchen. Mrs. David Russell, the owner who contacted me, felt nothing.

I promised to look into the "Ocean-Born" Mary haunting the first chance I got. Halloween or about that time would be all right with me, and I wouldn't wait around for any coach!

"There is a lady medium I think you should know," Mrs. Russell said when I spoke of bringing a psychic with me. "She saw Mary the very first time she came here."

My curiosity aroused, I communicated with the lady. She asked that I not use her married name, although she was not so shy several months after our visit to the house, when she gave a two-part interview to a Boston newspaper columnist. (Needless to say, the interview was not authorized by me, since I never allow mediums I work with to talk about their cases for publication. Thus Lorrie shall remain without a family name and anyone wishing to reach this medium will have to do so without my help.)

Lorrie wrote me she would be happy to serve the cause of truth, and I could count on her. There was nothing she wanted in return.

We did not get up to New Hampshire that Halloween. Mr. Russell had to have an operation, the house was unheated in the winter except for Mr. Roy's room, and New England winters are cold enough to freeze any ghost.

Although there was a caretaker at the time to look after the house and Mr. Roy upstairs, the Russells did not stay at the house in the winter, but made their home in nearby Chelmsford, Massachusetts.

I wrote Mrs. Russell postponing the investigation until spring. Mrs. Russell accepted my decision with some disappointment, but she was willing to wait. After all, the ghost at "Ocean-Born" Mary's house is not a malicious type. Mary Wallace just lived there, ever since she died in 1814, and you can't call a lady who likes to hold on to what is hers an intruder.

"We don't want to drive her out," Mrs. Russell repeatedly said to me. "After all, it *is* her house!"

Not many haunted-house owners make statements like that.

But something had happened at the house since our last conversation.

"Our caretaker dropped a space heater all the way down the stairs at the 'Ocean-Born' Mary house, and when it reached the bottom, the kerosene and the flames started to burn the stairs and climb the wall. There was no water in the house, so my husband went out after snow. While I stood there looking at the fire and powerless to do anything about it, the fire went right out all by itself right in front of my eyes; when my husband got back with the snow it was out. It was just as if someone *had smothered it with a blanket.*"

This was in December of 1963. I tried to set a new date, as soon as possible, and February 22 seemed possible. This time I would bring Bob Kennedy of WBZ, Boston, and the "Contact" producer Squire Rushnell with me to record my investigation.

Lorrie was willing, asking only that her name not be mentioned.

"I don't want anyone to know about my being different from them," she explained. "When I was young my family used to accuse me of spying because I knew things from the pictures I saw when I touched objects."

Psychometry, I explained, is very common among psychics, and nothing to be ashamed of.

I thought it was time to find out more about Lorrie's experiences at the haunted house.

"I first saw the house in September of 1961," she began. "It was on a misty, humid day, and there was a haze over the fields."

Strange, I thought, I always get my best psychic results when the atmosphere is moist.

Lorrie, who was in her early forties, was Vermont born and raised; she was married and had one daughter, Pauline. She was a tall redhead with sparkling eyes, and, come to think of it, not unlike the accepted picture of the ghostly Mary Wallace. Coincidence?

A friend of Lorrie's had seen the eerie house and suggested she go and see it also. That was all Lorrie knew about it, and she did not really expect anything uncanny to occur. Mr. Roy showed Lorrie and her daughter through the house and nothing startling happened. They left and started to walk down the entrance steps, crossing the garden in front of the house, and had reached the gate when Pauline clutched at her mother's arm and said:

"Mamma, what is that?"

Lorrie turned to look back at the house. In the upstairs window, a woman stood and looked out at them. Lorrie's husband was busy with the family car. Eventually, she called out to him, but as he turned to look, the apparition was gone.

She did not think of it again, and the weeks went by. But the house kept intruding itself into her thoughts more and more. Finally she could not restrain herself any longer, and returned to the house — even though it was 120 miles from her home in Weymouth, Massachusetts.

She confessed her extraordinary experience to the owner, and together they examined the house from top to bottom. She finally returned home.

She promised Roy she would return on All Hallow's Eve to see if the legend of Mary Wallace had any basis of fact. Unfortunately, word of her intentions got out, and when she finally arrived at the house, she had to sneak in the back to avoid the sensation-hungry press outside. During the days between her second visit and Halloween, the urge to go to Henniker kept getting stronger, as if someone were possessing her.

By that time the Russells were negotiating to buy the house, and Lorrie came up with them. Nothing happened to her that Halloween night. Perhaps she was torn between fear and a desire to fight the influence that had brought her out to Henniker to begin with.

Mediums, to be successful, must learn to relax and not allow their own notions to rule them. All through the following winter and summer, Lorrie fought the desire to return to "Ocean-Born" Mary's house. To no avail. She returned time and again, sometimes alone and sometimes with a friend.

Things got out of hand one summer night when she was home alone.

Exhausted from her last visit — the visits always left her an emotional wreck — she went to bed around 9:30 P.M.

"What happened that night?" I interjected. She seemed shaken even now.

"At 11 P.M., Mr. Holzer," Lorrie replied, "I found myself driving on the expressway, wearing my pajamas and robe, with no shoes or slippers, or money, or even a handkerchief. I was ten miles from my home and heading for Henniker. Terrified, I turned around and returned home, only to find my house ablaze with light, the doors open as I had left them, and the garage lights on. I must have left in an awful hurry."

"Have you found out why you are being pulled back to that house?"

She shook her head.

"No idea. But I've been back twice, even after that. I just can't seem to stay away from that house."

I persuaded her that perhaps there was a job to be done in that house, and the ghost wanted her to do it.

We did not go to Henniker in February, because of bad weather. We tried to set a date in May, 1964. The people from WBZ decided Henniker was too far away from Boston and dropped out of the planning.

Summer came around, and I went to Europe instead of Henniker. However, the prospect of a visit in the fall was very much in my mind.

It seemed as if someone were keeping me away from the house very much in the same way someone was pulling Lorrie toward it!

Come October, and we were really on our way, at last. Owen Lake, a public relations man who dabbles in psychic matters, introduced himself as "a friend" of mine and told Lorrie he'd come along, too. I had never met the gentleman, but in the end he could not make it anyway. So just four of us — my wife Catherine and I, Lorrie, and her nice, even-tempered husband, who had volunteered to drive us up to New Hampshire — started out from Boston. It was close to Halloween, all right, only two days before. If Mary Wallace were out haunting the countryside in her coach, we might very well run into her. The coach is out of old Irish folktales; it appears in numerous ghost stories of the Ould Sod. I'm sure that in the telling and retelling of the tale of Mary and her pirate, the coach got added.

The countryside is beautiful in a New England fall. As we rolled toward the New Hampshire state line, I asked Lorrie some more questions.

"When you first saw the ghost of 'Ocean-Born' Mary at the window of the house, Lorrie," I said, "what did she look like?"

"A lovely lady in her thirties, with auburn-colored hair, smiling rather intensely and thoughtfully. She stayed there for maybe three minutes, and then suddenly, *she just wasn't there.*"

"What about her dress?"

"It was a white dress."

Lorrie never saw an apparition of Mary again, but whenever she touched anything in the Henniker house, she received an impression of what the house was like when Mary had it, and she had felt her near the big fireplace several times.

Did she ever get an impression of what it was Mary wanted?

"She was a quick-tempered woman; I sensed that very strongly," Lorrie replied. "I have been to the house maybe twenty times altogether, and still don't know why. She just keeps pulling me there."

Lorrie had always felt the ghost's presence on these visits.

"One day I was walking among the bushes in the back of the house. I was wearing shorts, but I never got a scratch on my legs, because I kept feeling heavy skirts covering my legs. I could feel the brambles pulling at this invisible skirt I had on. I felt enveloped by something, or someone."

Mrs. Roy, the former owner's mother, had told of seeing the apparition many times, Lorrie stated.

"As a matter of fact, I have sensed her ghost in the house, too, but it is not a friendly wraith like Mary is."

Had she ever encountered this other ghost?

"Yes, my arm was grabbed one time by a malevolent entity,"

Lorrie said emphatically. "It was two years ago, and I was standing in what is now the living room, and my arm was taken by the elbow and pulled.

"I snatched my arm back, because I felt she was not friendly."

"What were you doing at the time that she might have objected to?"

"I really don't know."

Did she know of anyone else who had had an uncanny experience at the house?

"A strange thing happened to Mrs. Roy," Lorrie said. "A woman came to the house and said to her, 'What do you mean, the *rest* of the house?' The woman replied, 'Well, I was here yesterday, and a tall woman let me in and only showed me half of the house.' But, of course, there was nobody at the house that day."

What about the two state troopers? Could she elaborate on their experience?

"They met her walking down the road that leads to the house. She was wearing a Colonial-type costume, and they found that odd. Later they realized they had seen a ghost, especially as no one of her description lived in the house at the time."

Rudi D., Lorrie's husband, was a hospital technician. He was with her on two or three occasions when she visited the house. Did he ever feel anything special?

"The only thing unusual I ever felt at the house was that I wanted to get out of there fast," he said.

"The very first time we went up," Lorrie added, "something kept pulling me toward it, but my husband insisted we go back. There was an argument about our continuing the trip, when suddenly the door of the car flew open of its own volition. Somehow we decided to continue on to the house."

An hour later, we drove up a thickly overgrown hill and along a winding road at the end of which the "Ocean-Born" Mary house stood in solitary stateliness, a rectangular building of gray stone and brown trim, very well preserved.

We parked the car and walked across the garden that sets the house well back from the road. There was peace and autumn in the air. We were made welcome by Corinne Russell, her husband David, and two relatives who happened to be with them that day. Entering the main door beneath a magnificent early American eagle, we admired the fine wooden staircase leading to the upstairs — the staircase on which the mysterious fire had taken place — and then entered the room to the left of it, where the family had assembled around an old New England stove.

During the three years the Russells had lived at the house, nothing uncanny had happened to Mrs. Russell, except for the incident with the fire. David Russell, a man almost typical of the shrewd New England Yankee who weighs his every word, was willing to tell me about *his* experiences, however.

"The first night I ever slept in what we call the Lafayette room, upstairs, there was quite a thundershower on, and my dog and I were upstairs. I always keep my dog with me, on account of the boys coming around to do damage to the property.

"Just as I lay down in bed, I heard very heavy footsteps. They sounded to me to be in the two rooms which we had just restored, on the same floor. I was quite annoyed, almost frightened, and I went into the rooms, but there was nobody there or anywhere else in the house."

"Interesting," I said. "Was there more?"

"Now this happened only last summer. A few weeks later, when I was in that same room, I was getting undressed when I suddenly heard somebody pound on my door. I said to myself, "Oh, it's only the house settling," and I got into bed. A few minutes later, the door knob turned back and forth. I jumped out of bed, opened the door, and there was absolutely nobody there. The only other people in the house at the time were the invalid Mr. Roy, locked in his room, and my wife downstairs."

What about visual experiences?

"No, but I went to the cellar not long ago with my dog, about four in the afternoon, or rather tried to — this dog never leaves me, but on this particular occasion, something kept her from going with me into the cellar. Her hair stood up and she would not budge."

The Lafayette room, by the way, is the very room in which the pirate, Don Pedro, is supposed to have lived. The Russells did nothing to change the house structurally, only restored it as it had been and generally cleaned it up.

I now turned to Florence Harmon, an elderly neighbor of the Russells, who had some recollections about the house. Mrs. Harmon recalls the house when she herself was very young, long before the Russells came to live in it.

"Years later, I returned to the house and Mrs. Roy asked me whether I could help her locate 'the treasure' since I was reputed to be psychic."

Was there really a treasure?

"If there was, I think it was found," Mrs. Harmon said. "At the time Mrs. Roy talked to me, she also pointed out that there were two elm trees on the grounds — the only two elm trees around. They looked like some sort of markers to her. But before the Roys had the house, a Mrs. Morrow lived here. I know this from my uncle, who was a stone mason, and who built a vault for her."

I didn't think Mrs. Harmon had added anything material to knowledge of the treasure, so I thanked her and turned my attention to the other large room, on the right hand side of the staircase. Nicely furnished with period pieces, it boasted a fireplace flanked by sofas, and had a rectangular piano in the corner. The high windows were curtained on the sides, and one could see the New England landscape through them.

We seated ourselves around the fireplace and hoped that Mary would honor us with a visit. Earlier I had inspected the entire house, the hearthstone under which Don Pedro allegedly lay buried, and the small bedrooms upstairs where David Russell had heard the footsteps. Each of us had stood at the window in the corridor upstairs and stared out of it, very much the way the ghost must have done when she was observed by Lorrie and her daughter.

And now it was Mary's turn.

"This was her room," Lorrie explained, "and I do feel her presence." But she refused to go into trance, afraid to "let go." Communication would have to be via clairvoyance, with Lorrie as the interpreter. This was not what I had hoped for. Nevertheless we would try to evaluate whatever material we could obtain.

"Sheet and quill," Lorrie said now, and a piece of paper was handed her along with a pencil. Holding it on her lap, Lorrie was poised to write, if Mary wanted to use her hand, so to speak. The pencil suddenly jumped from Lorrie's hand with considerable force.

"Proper quill," the ghost demanded.

I explained about the shape of quills these days, and handed Lorrie my own pencil.

"Look, lady," Lorrie explained to the ghost. "I'll show you it writes. I'll write my name."

And she wrote in her own, smallish, rounded hand, "Lorrie."

There was a moment of silence. Evidently, the ghost was thinking it over. Then Lorrie's hand, seemingly not under her own control, wrote with a great deal of flourish "Mary Wallace." The "M" and "W" had curves and ornamentation typical of eighteenth-century calligraphy. It was not at all like Lorrie's own handwriting.

"Tell her to write some more. The quill is working," I commanded.

Lorrie seemed to be upset by something the ghost told her.

"No," she said. "I can't do that. No."

"What does she want?" I asked.

"She wants me to sleep, but I won't do it."

Trance, I thought — even the ghost demands it. It would have been so interesting to have Mary speak directly to us through Lorrie's entranced lips. You can lead a medium to the ghost, but you can't make her go under if she's scared.

Lorrie instead told the ghost to tell *her,* or to write through her. But no trance, thank you. Evidently, the ghost did not like to be told how to communicate. We waited. Then I suggested that Lorrie be very relaxed and it would be "like sleep" so the ghost could talk to us directly.

"She's very much like me, but not so well trimmed," the ghost said of Lorrie. Had she picked her to carry her message because of physical resemblance, I wondered.

"She's waiting for Young John," Lorrie now said. Not young John. The stress was on young. Perhaps it was one name — Young-john.

"It happened in the north pasture," Mary said through Lorrie now. "He killed Warren Langerford. The Frazier boys found the last bone."

I asked why it concerned her. Was she involved? But there was no reply.

Then the ghost of Mary introduced someone else standing next to her.

"Mrs. Roy is with her, because she killed her daughter," Lorrie said, hesitatingly, and added, on her own, "but I don't believe she did." Later we found out that the ghost was perhaps not lying, but of course nobody had any proof of such a crime — if it were indeed a crime.

"Why do you stay on in this house?" I asked.

"This house is my house, h-o-u-s-e!" "Ocean-Born" Mary reminded me.

"Do you realize you are what is commonly called dead?" I demanded. As so often with ghosts, the question brought on resistance to face reality. Mary seemed insulted and withdrew.

I addressed the ghost openly, offering to help her, and at the same time explaining her present position to her. This was her chance to speak up.

"She's very capricious," Lorrie said. "When you said you'd bring her peace, she started to laugh."

But Mary was gone, for the present anyway.

We waited, and tried again a little later. This time Lorrie said she heard a voice telling her to come back tonight.

"We can't," I decided. "If she wants to be helped, it will have to be now."

Philip Babb, the pirate's real name (as I discovered later), allegedly had built a secret passage under the house. The Russells were still looking for it. There were indeed discrepancies in the thickness of some of the walls, and there were a number of secret holes that didn't lead anywhere. But no passage. Had the pirate taken his secrets to his grave?

I found our experience at Henniker singularly unsatisfactory since no real evidence had been forthcoming from the ghost herself. No doubt another visit would have to be made, but I didn't mind that at all. "Ocean-Born" Mary's place was a place one can easily visit time and again. The rural charm of the place and the timeless atmosphere of the old house made it a first-rate tourist attraction. Thousands of people came to the house every year.

We returned to New York and I thought no more about it until I received a letter from James Caron, who had heard me discuss the house on the "Contact" program in Boston. He had been to the house in quest of pirate lore and found it very much haunted.

James Caron was in the garage business at Bridgewater, Massachusetts. He had a high school and trade school education, and was married, with two children. Searching for stories of buried treasure and pirates was a hobby of his, and he sometimes lectured on it. He had met Gus Roy about six years before. Roy complained that his deceased mother was trying to contact him for some reason. Her picture kept falling off the wall where it was hung, and he constantly felt "a presence." Would Mr. Caron know of a good medium?

In August of 1959, James Caron brought a spiritualist named Paul Amsdent to the "Ocean-Born" Mary house. Present at the ensuing séance were Harold Peters, a furniture salesman; Hugh Blanchard, a lawyer; Ernest Walbourne, a fireman, and brother-in-law of Caron; Gus Roy; and Mr. Caron himself. Tape recording the séance, Caron had trouble with his equipment. Strange sounds kept intruding. Unfortunately, there was among those present someone with hostility toward psychic work, and Gus Roy's mother did not manifest. However, something else did happen.

"There appear to be people buried somewhere around or in the house," the medium Amsdent said, "enclosed by a stone wall of some sort."

I thought of the hearthstone and of Mrs. Harmon's vault. Coincidence?

Mr. Caron used metal detectors all over the place to satisfy Gus Roy that there was no "pirate treasure" buried in or near the house.

A little later, James Caron visited the house again. This time he was accompanied by Mrs. Caron and Mr. and Mrs. Walbourne. Both ladies were frightened by the sound of a heavy door opening and closing with no one around and no air current in the house.

Mrs. Caron had a strong urge to go to the attic, but Mr. Caron stopped her. Ernest Walbourne, a skeptic, was alone in the so-called "death" room upstairs, looking at some pictures stacked in a corner. Suddenly, he clearly heard a female voice telling him to get out of the house. He looked around, but there was nobody upstairs. Frightened, he left the house at once and later required medication for a nervous condition!

Again, things quieted down as far as "Ocean-Born" Mary was concerned, until I saw a lengthy story — two parts, in fact — in the *Boston Record-American*, in which my erstwhile medium Lorrie had let her hair down to columnist Harold Banks.

It seemed that Lorrie could not forget Henniker, after all. With publicist Owen Lake, she returned to the house in November, 1964, bringing with her some oil of wintergreen, which she claimed Mary Wallace asked her to bring along.

Two weeks later, the report went on, Lorrie felt Mary Wallace in her home in Weymouth near Boston. Lorrie was afraid that Mary Wallace might "get into my body and use it for whatever purpose she wants to. I might wake up some day and *be* Mary Wallace."

That's the danger of being a medium without proper safeguards. They tend to identify with a personality that has come through them. Especially when they read all there is in print about them.

I decided to take someone to the house who knew nothing about it, someone who was not likely to succumb to the wiles of amateur "ESP experts," inquisitive columnists and such, someone who would do exactly what I required of her: Sybil Leek, famed British psychic.

It was a glorious day late in spring when we arrived at "Ocean-Born" Mary's house in a Volkswagen station wagon driven by two alert young students from Goddard College in Vermont: Jerry Weener and Jay Lawrence. They had come to Boston to fetch us and take us all the way up to their campus, where I was to address the students and faculty. I proposed that they drive us by way of Henniker, and the two young students of parapsychology agreed enthusiastically. It was their first experience with an actual séance and they brought with them a lively dose of curiosity.

Sybil Leek brought with her something else: "Mr. Sasha," a healthy four-foot boa constrictor someone had given her for a pet. At first I thought she was kidding when she spoke with tender care of her snake, coiled peacefully in his little basket. But practical Sybil, author of some nine books, saw still another possibility in "Life with Sasha" and for that reason kept the snake on with her. On the way to Henniker, the car had a flat tire and we took this opportunity to get acquainted with Sasha, as Sybil gave him a run around the New Hampshire countryside.

Although I have always had a deep-seated dislike for anything reptilian, snakes, serpents, and other slitherers, terrestrial or maritime, I must confess that I found this critter less repulsive than I had thought he would be. At any rate, "Mr. Sasha" was collected once more and carefully replaced in his basket and the journey continued to Henniker, where the Russells were expecting us with great anticipation.

After a delightful buffet luncheon — "Mr. Sasha" had his the week before, as snakes are slow digesters — we proceeded to the large room upstairs to the right of the entrance door, commonly called the Lafayette room, and Sybil took the chair near the fireplace. The rest of us — the Russells, a minister friend of theirs, two neighbors, my wife Catherine and I, and our two student friends — gathered around her in a circle.

It was early afternoon. The sun was bright and clear. It didn't seem like it would be a good day for ghosts. Still, we had come to have a talk with the elusive Mary Wallace in her own domain, and if I knew Sybil, she would not disappoint us. Sybil is a very powerful medium, and something *always* happens.

Sybil knew nothing about the house since I had told our hosts not to discuss it with her before the trance session. I asked her if she had any clairvoyant impressions about the house.

"My main impressions were outside," Sybil replied, "near where the irises are. I was drawn to that spot and felt very strange. There is something outside this house which means more than things inside!"

"What about inside the house? What do you feel here?"

"The most impressive room I think is the loom room," Sybil said, and I thought, that's where Ernest Walbourne heard the voice telling him to get out, in the area that's also called the "death" room.

"They don't want us here . . . there is a conflict between two people . . . somebody wants something he can't have . . ."

Presently, Sybil was in trance. There was a moment of silence as I waited anxiously for the ghost of Mary Wallace to manifest itself through Sybil. The first words coming from the lips of the entranced medium were almost unintelligible.

Gradually, the voice became clearer and I had her repeat the words until I could be sure of them.

"Say-mon go to the lion's head," she said now. "To the lion's head. Be careful."

"Why should I be careful?"

"In case he catches you."

"Who are you?"

"Mary Degan."

"What are you doing here?"

"Waiting. Someone fetch me."

She said *"Witing"* with a strong cockney accent, and suddenly I realized that the *"say-mon"* was probably a seaman.

"Whose house is this?" I inquired.

"Daniel Burn's." (Perhaps it was "Birch.")

"What year is this?"

"1798."

"Who built this house?"

"Burn . . ."

"How did you get here?"

"All the time, come and go . . . to hide . . . I have to wait. He wants the money. Burn. Daniel Burn."

I began to wonder what had happened to Mary Wallace. Who was this new member of the ghostly cast? Sybil knew nothing whatever of a pirate or a pirate treasure connected by legend to this house. Yet her very first trance words concerned *a seaman and money*.

Did Mary Degan have someone else with her, I hinted. Maybe this was only the first act and the lady of the house was being coy in time for a second act appearance.

But the ghost insisted that she was Mary Degan and that she lived here, "with the old idiot."

"Who was the old idiot?" I demanded.

"Mary," the Degan girl replied.

"What is Mary's family name?"

"Birch," she replied without hesitation.

I looked at Mrs. Russell, who shook her head. Nobody knew of Mary Wallace by any other name. Had she had another husband we did not know about?

Was there anyone else with her, I asked.

"Mary Birch, Daniel, and Jonathan," she replied.

"Who is Jonathan?"

"Jonathan Harrison Flood," the ghostly girl said.

A week or so later, I checked with my good friend Robert Nesmith, expert in pirate lore. Was there a pirate by that name? There had been, but his date is given as 1610, far too early for our man. But then Flood was a very common name. Also, this Flood might have used another name as his *nom de pirate* and Flood might have been his real, civilian name.

"What are they doing in this house?" I demanded.

"They come to look for their money," Sybil in trance replied. "The old idiot took it."

"What sort of money was it?"

"Dutch money," came the reply. "Very long ago."

"Who brought the money to this house?"

"Mary. Not me."

"Whose money was it?"

"Johnny's."

"How did he get it?"

"Very funny . . . he helped himself . . . so we did."

"What profession did he have?"

"Went down to the sea. Had a lot of funny business. Then he got caught, you know. So they did him in."

"Who did him in?"

"The runners. In the bay."

"What year was that?"

"Ninety-nine."

"What happened to the money after that?"

"She hid it. Outside. Near the lion's head."

"Where is the lion's head?"

"You go down past the little rocks, in the middle of the rocks, a little bit like a lion's head."

"If I left this house by the front entrance, which way would I turn?"

"The right, down past the little rock on the right. Through the trees, down the little . . . "

"How far from the house?"

"Three minutes."

"Is it under the rock?"

"Lion's head."

"How far below?"

"As big as a boy."

"What will I find there?"

"The gold. Dutch gold."

"Anything else?"

"No, unless she put it there."

"Why did she put it there?"

"Because he came back for it."

"What did she do?"

"She said it was hers. Then he went away. Then they caught him, and good thing, too. He never came back and she went off, too."

"When did she leave here?"

"Eighteen three."

"What was she like? Describe her."

"Round, not as big as me, dumpy thing, she thought she owned everything."

"How was Jonathan related to Daniel?"

"Daniel stayed here when Johnny went away and then they would divide the money, but they didn't because of Mary. She took it."

"Did you see the money?"

"I got some money. Gold. It says 1747."

"Is anyone buried in this ground?"

"Sometimes they brought them back here when they got killed down by the river."

"Who is buried in the house?"

"I think Johnny."

I now told Mary Degan to fetch me the other Mary, the lady of the house. But the girl demurred. The other Mary did not like to talk to strangers.

"What do *you* look like?" I asked. I still was not sure if Mary Wallace was not masquerading as her own servant girl to fool us.

"Skinny and tall."

"What do you wear?"

"A gray dress."

"What is your favorite spot in this house?"

"The little loom room. Peaceful."

"Do you always stay there?"

"No." The voice was proud now. "I go where I want."

"Whose house is this?" Perhaps I could trap her if she was indeed Mary Wallace.

"Mary Birch."

"Has she got a husband?"

"They come and go. There's always company here — that's why I go to the loom room."

I tried to send her away, but she wouldn't go.

"Nobody speaks to me," she complained. "Johnny . . . she won't let him speak to me. Nobody is going to send me away."

"Is there a sea captain in this house?" I asked.

She almost shouted the reply.

"*Johnny!*"

"Where is he from?"

"Johnny is from the island."

She then explained that the trouble with Johnny and Mary was about the sea. Especially about the money the captain had.

"Will the money be found?" I asked.

"Not until I let it."

I asked Mary Degan to find me Mary Wallace. No dice. The lady wanted to be coaxed. Did she want some presents, I asked. That hit a happier note.

"Brandy . . . some clothes," she said. "She needs some hair . . . hasn't got much hair."

"Ask her if she could do with some oil of wintergreen," I said, sending up a trial balloon.

"She's got a bad back," the ghost said, and I could tell from the surprised expression on Mrs. Russell's face that Mary Wallace had indeed had a bad back.

"She makes it . . . people bring her things . . . rub her back . . . back's bad . . . she won't let you get the money . . . not yet . . . may want to build another house, in the garden . . . in case she needs it . . . sell it . . . she knows she is not what she used to be because her back's bad . . . she'll never go. Not now."

I assured her that the Russells wanted her to stay as long as she liked. After all, it was her house, too.

"Where is Johnny's body buried?" I now asked.

"Johnny's body," she murmured, "is under the fireplace."

Nobody had told Sybil about the persistent rumors that the old pirate lay under the hearthstone.

"Don't tell anyone," she whispered.

"How deep?"

"Had to be deep."

"Who put him there?"

"I shan't tell you."

"Did you bury anything with him?"

"I shan't tell. He is no trouble now. Poor Johnny."

"How did Johnny meet Mary?"

"I think they met on a ship."

"Ocean-Born" Mary, I thought. Sybil did not even know the name of the house, much less the story of how it got that name.

"All right," I said. "Did Mary have any children?"

"Four . . . in the garden. You can never tell with her."

"Did anyone kill anyone in this house at any time?"

"Johnny was killed, you know. Near the money. The runners chased him and he was very sick, we thought he was dead, and then he came here. I think she pushed him when he hurt his leg. We both brought him back here and put him under the fireplace. I didn't think he was dead."

"But you buried him anyway?" I said.

"She did," the ghost servant replied. "Better gone, she said. He's only come back for the money."

"Then Mary and Johnny weren't exactly friendly?"

"They were once."

"What changed things?"

"The money. She took his money. The money he fought for. Fighting money."

Suddenly, the tone of voice of the servant girl changed.

"I want to go outside," she begged. "She watches me. I can go out because her back is bad today. Can't get up, you see. So I can go out."

I promised to help her.

Suspiciously, she asked, "What do you want?"

"Go outside. You are free to go," I intoned.

"Sit on the rocks," the voice said. "If she calls out? She can get very angry."

"I will protect you," I promised.

"She says there are other places under the floor . . ." the girl ghost added, suddenly.

"Any secret passages?" I asked.

"Yes. Near the old nursery. First floor. Up the stairs, the loom room, the right hand wall. You can get out in the smoke room!"

Mr. Russell had told me of his suspicions that on structural evidence alone there was a hidden passage behind the smoke room. How would Sybil know this? Nobody had discussed it with her or showed her the spot.

I waited for more. But she did not know of any other passages, except one leading to the rear of the house.

"What about the well?"

"She did not like that either, because she thought *he* put his money there."

"Did he?"

"Perhaps he did. She used to put money in one place, he into another, and I think he put some money into the smoke room. He was always around there. Always watching each other. Watch me, too. Back of the house used to be where he could hide. People always looking for Johnny. Runners."

"Who was Mr. Birch?"

"Johnny had a lot to do with his house, but he was away a lot and so there was always some man here while he was away."

"Who paid for the house originally?"

"I think Johnny."

"Why did he want this house?"

"When he got enough money, he would come here and stay forever. He could not stay long ever, went back to the sea, and she came."

I tried another tack.

"Who was Don Pedro?" That was the name given the pirate in the popular tale.

She had heard the name, but could not place it.

"What about Mary Wallace?"

"Mary Wallace was Mary *Birch,*" the ghost said, as if correcting me. "She had several names."

"Why?"

"Because she had several husbands."

Logical enough, if true.

"Wallace lived here a little while, I think," she added.

"Who was first, Wallace or Birch?"

"Birch. Mary Wallace, Mary Birch, is good enough."

Did the name Philip Babb mean anything to her? That allegedly was the pirate's real name.

"She had a little boy named Philip," the ghost said, and I thought, why not? After all, they had named Mary for the pirate's mother, why not reciprocate and name *her* son for the old man? Especially with all that loot around.

"If I don't go now, she'll wake up," the girl said. "Philip Babb, Philip Babb, he was somewhere in the back room. That was his room. I remember him."

How did Philip get on with Johnny? I wanted to know if they were one and the same person or not.

"Not so good," the ghost said. "Johnny did not like men here, you know."

I promised to watch out for Mary, and sent the girl on her way.

I then brought Sybil out of trance.

A few moments later, we decided to start our treasure hunt in the garden, following the instructions given us by Mary Degan, girl ghost.

Sybil was told nothing more than to go outside and let her intuition lead her toward any spot she thought important. The rest of us followed her like spectators at the National Open Golf Tournament.

We did not have to walk far. About twenty yards from the house, near some beautiful iris in bloom, we located the three stones. The one in the middle looked indeed somewhat like a lion's head, when viewed at a distance. I asked the others in the group to look at it. There was no doubt about it. If there was a lion's head on the grounds, this was it. What lay underneath? What indeed was underneath the hearthstone in the house itself?

The Russells promised to get a mine detector to examine the areas involved. If there was metal in the ground, the instrument would show it. Meanwhile, the lore about "Ocean-Born" Mary had been enriched by the presence in the nether world of Mary Degan, servant girl, and the intriguing picture of two pirates — Johnny and Philip Babb. Much of this is very difficult to trace. But the fact is that Sybil Leek, who came to Henniker a total stranger, was able, in trance, to tell about a man at sea, a Mary, a pirate treasure, hidden passages, a child named Philip, four children of Mary, and the presence of a ghost in the loom room upstairs. All of this had been checked.

Why should not the rest be true also? Including, perhaps, the elusive treasure?

Only time will tell.

The Ghosts of Barbery Lane

"*I* know a house in Rye, New York, with a ghost," painter Mary Melikian said to me, and there was pleasure in her voice at being the harbinger of good news. Mary knew how eager I was to find a haunted house, preferably one that was still haunted.

"A ghost," Mary repeated and added, tantalizingly, "a ghost that *likes to slam doors.*"

I pumped Mary for details. One of her friends was the celebrated portrait painter Molly Guion, known in Rye as Mrs. John Smythe. Molly and her husband, an architect, lived in a sprawling mid-nineteenth-century house atop a bluff overlooking the old New Haven Railroad bed, surrounded by houses built in later years. The Smythes' house was the first one on the tract, the original Manor House, built there around 1860 by one Jared B. Peck.

I arranged with Mrs. Smythe to visit the house the following week, in August of 1963. My wife Catherine and I were met at the train by Mrs. Smythe, whose husband also came along to welcome us. The drive to the house (originally called "The Cedars" but now only known as a number on Barbery Lane) took less than five minutes, yet you might well have entered another world — so serene and rural was the atmosphere that greeted us that moonlit evening, when the station wagon pulled up to the gleaming-white 100-year-old house the Smythes had called home since the summer of 1957.

Rising to four floors, the structure reminded me of the stylized paintings of Victorian houses associated with another world. A wide porch went around it at the ground level, and shady trees protected it from view and intrusion.

The huge living room was tastefully furnished with fine antiques and all over the house we encountered the marvelously alive portraits painted by Molly Guion, which blended naturally into the decor of the house. This was a stately mansion, only an hour from New York but as quiet and removed from the city of subways as if it stood in the Deep South or Down East. We seated ourselves comfortably. Then I came right to the point.

"This ghost," I began. "What exactly does it do and when did you first notice anything unusual in the house?"

This is my standard opener. Molly Guion was more than happy to tell us everything. Her husband left for a while to tend to some chores.

"We arrived in this house on a hot summer day in 1957 — in July," she recalled. "About a week later — I remember it was a particularly hot night — we heard a door slam. Both my husband and I heard it."

"Well?"

"But there was absolutely nobody in the house at the time except us," Molly said, significantly. "We heard it many times after that. Maybe six or seven separate instances. Once around ten o'clock at night I heard the front door open and close again with a characteristic squeak. Mother was living with us then and I was not feeling well, so that a nurse was staying with me. I called out 'Mother,' thinking she had come home a bit early, but there was no reply. Since then I've heard the front door open many times, but there is never anyone there."

"Is it the front door then?"

"No, not always. Sometimes it is the front door and sometimes it is this door on the second floor. Come, I'll show you."

Molly led us up the winding stairs to a second floor containing many small rooms, all exquisitely furnished with the solid furniture of the Victorian period. There was a tiny room on one side of the corridor leading to the rear of the house, and across from it, the door that was heard to slam. It was a heavy wooden door, leading to a narrow winding staircase which in turn led up another flight of stairs to the third floor. Here Molly Guion had built herself a magnificent studio, taking up most of the floor space.

"One day in January of 1962," she volunteered, "I was downstairs in the kitchen talking to an exterminator, when I heard a door slam hard — it seemed to me. Yet, there was no one in the house at the time, only we two downstairs."

"Outside of yourself and your husband, has anyone else heard these uncanny noises?"

Molly nodded quickly.

"There was this colored man that worked for me. He said, 'Mrs. Smythe, every time I'm alone in the house, I hear a door slam!'"

"Anyone else?"

"A Scottish cleaning woman, name of Roberta Gillan. She lives in Harrison, New York. She once came to me and said, 'Did you just slam a door?' Of course, I hadn't."

We were now seated in a small room off the second-floor corridor. The light was moody and the air dank. There was a quietness around the house so heavy I almost *wished* I could hear a door slam. Molly had more to reveal.

"Once, a little girl named Andree, age eleven, came to visit us and within seconds exclaimed — 'Mamma, there is a ghost in this house!'"

Our hostess admitted to being somewhat psychic, with sometimes comical results. Years ago, when a boyfriend had failed to keep their date, she saw him clearly in a dream-vision with a certain blonde girl. He later explained his absence in a casual way, but she nailed him with a description of his blonde — and he confessed the truth.

Two years after she moved into the house, Molly developed a case of asthma, the kind very old people sometimes suffer from. Strangely, it bothered her only in certain rooms and not at all in others. It started like a kind of allergy, and gradually worsened until it became a fully grown asthmatic condition. Although two rooms were side by side, sleeping in one would aggravate the condition, but sleeping in the other made her completely free of it!

"Did you hear any other noises — I mean, outside of the door slamming?" I asked.

"Yes. Not so long ago we had a dinner party here, and among the guests was a John Gardner, a vice president of the Bankers Trust Company."

Suddenly she had heard someone rap at the window of the big room downstairs. They tried to ignore the noise, but Gardner heard it too.

"Is someone rapping at your window?" he inquired.

He was assured it was nothing. Later he took Molly aside and remonstrated with her. "I distinctly heard the raps," he said. Molly just smiled.

Finally the Smythes called on the American Society for Psychic Research to find an explanation for all these goings-on. But the Society was in no hurry to do anything about the case. They suggested Molly write them a letter, which she did, but they still took no action.

I thoroughly inspected the premises — walked up the narrow staircase into Molly Guion's studio where some of the best portrait oils hung. Her paintings of famous Britons had just toured as an exhibition and the house was full of those she owned (the greater part of her work was commissioned and scattered in collections, museums, and private homes).

There was a tiny bedroom next to the landing in back of the studio, evidently a servant's room, since the entire floor had originally been servants' quarters. The house had sixteen rooms in all.

By now Mr. Smythe had joined us and I explained my mission. Had he ever noticed anything unusual about the house?

"Oh yes," he volunteered, speaking slowly and deliberately. "There are all sorts of noises in this house and they're not ordinary noises — I mean, the kind you can *explain*."

"For instance?"

"I was sleeping up here one night in the little bedroom here," he said, pointing to the servant's room in back of the landing, "when I heard footsteps. They were the steps of an older person."

But there was no one about, he asserted.

Jared Peck, who built the house in 1860, died in 1895, and the house passed into the hands of his estate to be rented to various tenants. In 1910, Stuyvesant Wainwright bought the property. In the following year, his ex-wife, now Mrs. Catlin, bought it from him and lived in it until her death in the 1920s.

The former Mrs. Wainwright turned out to be a colorful person. Born wealthy, she had a very short temper and the servants never stayed long in her house.

"She certainly liked to slam doors," Mr. Smythe observed. "I mean she was the kind of person who would do that sort of thing."

"One day she became very ill and everybody thought she would die," Molly related. "There she was stretched out on this very couch and the doctor felt free to talk about her condition. 'She won't last much longer,' he said, and shrugged. Mrs. Wainwright sat up with a angry jolt and barked, 'I intend to!' And she did, for many more years of hot-tempered shenanigans."

In her later years Mrs. Wainwright moved to the former servants' quarters on the second floor — whether out of economy or for reasons of privacy no one knows for sure. The *slamming door* was right in the heart of her rooms and no doubt she traveled up those narrow stairs to the floor above many times.

The plumber, painter, and carpenter who worked for Mrs. Wainwright were still living in Rye and they all remembered her as a willful and headstrong woman who liked to have her own way. Her granddaughter, Mrs. Condit, recalled her vividly. The Smythes were pretty sure that Mrs. Wainwright slept up there on the second floor — they found a screen marked "My bedroom window" that fit no other window in any of the rooms.

The Smythes acquired the handsome house from the next owner, one Arthur Flemming, who used Mrs. Wainwright's old room. But he didn't experience anything unusual, or at any rate said nothing about it.

There was a big theft once in the house and Mrs. Wainwright may have been worried about it. Strongly attached to worldly possessions, she kept valuables in various trunks on the third floor, and ran up to look at them from time to time to make sure everything was still there.

Could the slamming of the door be a re-enactment of these frequent nervous expeditions up the stairs? Could the opening and closing of the entrance door be a fearful examination of the door to see if the lock was secure, or if there was anyone strange lurking about outside?

The very day after our visit to this haunted house, a young painter friend of Molly's named Helen Charleton, of Bronxville, New York, was alone in the studio that Molly let her use occasionally to do some painting of her own. She was quite alone in the big house when she clearly heard the front door open. Calling out, she received no answer. Thinking that the gardener might have a key, and that she might be in danger, she took hold of what heavy objects she could put her hands on and waited anxiously for the steps that were sure to resound any moment. No steps came. An hour later, the doorbell rang and she finally dashed down to the entrance door. *The door was tightly shut,* and no one was about. Yet she *had* heard the characteristic noise of the opening of the old-fashioned door!

The mailman's truck was just pulling away, so she assumed it was he who had rung the bell. Just then Molly returned.

"I've heard the door slam many times," Helen Charleton said to me, "and it always sounds so far away. I think it's on the first floor, but I can't be sure."

Was Mrs. Wainwright still walking the Victorian corridors of "The Cedars," guarding her treasures upstairs?

When Catherine and I returned from Europe in the fall of 1964, Molly Guion had news for us. All was far from quiet in Rye. In the upstairs room where Molly's invalid mother was bedridden, a knob had flown off a table while Mrs. Guion stood next to it. In the presence of a nurse, the bathroom lights had gone on and off by themselves. More sinister, a heavy ashtray had taken off on its own to sail clear across the room. A door had opened by itself, and footsteps had been heard again.

A new nurse had come, and the number of witnesses who had heard or seen uncanny goings-on was now eight.

I decided it was time for a séance, and on January 6, 1965, medium Ethel Meyers, Mary Melikian, Catherine and I took a New Haven train for Rye, where John Smythe picked us up in his station wagon.

While Ethel Meyers waited in the large sitting room downstairs, I checked on the house and got the latest word on the hauntings. Molly Guion took me to the kitchen to show me the spot where one of the most frightening incidents had taken place.

"Last Christmas, my mother, my husband, and I were here in the kitchen having lunch, and right near us on a small table next to the wall was a great big bread knife. Suddenly, to our amazement, *the knife took off into the air,* performed an arc in the air and landed about a yard away from the table. This was about noon, in good light."

"Was that the only time something like this happened?"

"The other day the same thing happened. We were down in the kitchen again at nighttime. My husband and I heard a terrific crash upstairs. It was in the area of the servants' quarters on the second floor, which is in the area where that door keeps slamming. I went up to investigate and found a heavy ashtray lying on the floor about a yard away from the table in my husband's den."

"And there was no one upstairs — flesh-and-blood, that is?"

"No. The object could not have just slipped off the table. It landed some distance away."

"Amazing," I conceded. "Was there more?"

"Last week I was standing in the upstairs sitting room with one of the nurses, when a piece of a chair that was lying in the center of a table took off and landed in the middle of the floor."

"Before your eyes?"

"Before our eyes."

"What would you say is the most frequent phenomenon here?" I asked.

"The opening of the front door downstairs. We and others have heard this characteristic noise any number of times, and there is never anyone there."

I turned to Mrs. Witty, the nurse currently on duty with Molly Guion's mother.

"How long have you been in this house?"

"Since October, 1964."

"Have you noticed anything unusual in these four months?"

"Well, Mrs. Smythe and I were in the patient's bedroom upstairs, when we heard the front door downstairs open. I remarked to Mrs. Smythe that she had a visitor, and went down to the front door, and looked. *The heavy chain was swinging loose, and the front door was slightly ajar!*"

"Did you see any visitor?"

"No. I opened the door, looked all around, but there was no one there."

"Anything else?"

"A couple of weeks later, the same thing happened. I was alone in the house with the patient, and the door was locked securely. An hour after I had myself locked it, I heard the door shut tightly, but the chain was again swinging by itself."

I next turned to Mr. Smythe to check up on his own experiences since we had last talked. Mr. Smythe was a naval architect and very cautious in his appraisal of the uncanny. He was still hearing the "measured steps" in the attic room where he sometimes slept, even when he was all alone in the house.

I returned to Ethel Meyers, the medium, who had seated herself in a large chair in the front sitting room downstairs.

"Anything happening?" I asked, for I noticed a peculiar expression on Ethel's face, as if she were observing something or someone.

"I picture a woman clairvoyantly," Ethel said. "She looks at me with a great deal of defiance."

"Why are you pointing across the room at that sofa?" I asked my wife.

"I saw a light from the corner of my eye and I thought it was a car, but no car has passed by," Catherine said.

If a car *had* passed by, no reflection could have been seen at that spot, since no window faced in that direction.

While Ethel prepared for the trance sitting, I went outside the room to talk to Georgia Anne Warren, a young dancer who had modeled for some of Molly Guion's paintings. Her full-length nude study graced the studio upstairs, and there amid the Churchill portraits and faces of the famous or near-famous, it was like a shining beacon of beauty. But Miss Warren wasn't only posing for a painter, we discovered — she was also modeling for a ghost.

"I heard a thumping noise, as if someone were going upstairs. I was in the kitchen. The steps sounded as if they were coming from the dining room. There was no one coming in. The only people in the house at the time were Molly Guion and myself. No doubt about it."

I thanked the redheaded model and followed Ethel Meyers up the stairs, to which she seemed propelled by a sudden impulse. There, on the winding Victorian steps, Ethel made her first contact with the ghost.

"Make the body very cold. Don't put it in the ground when it's warm. Let it get very cold!" she mumbled, as if not quite herself.

"Let her speak through you," I suggested.

"She is," Ethel replied, and continued in a somewhat strange voice. "Ring around the rosies, a pocketful of posies . . . "

I turned toward the stairwell and asked the ghost to communicate with us, tell her tale, and find help through us. There was no further answer.

I led Mrs. Meyers back to her chair, and asked Molly Guion to dim the lights a little so we could all relax. Meanwhile, other witnesses had arrived. They included *New York Times* reporter N. Berkowitz, Benton & Bowles vice-president Gordon Webber, publicist Bill Ryan, and book critic John K. Hutchins. We formed a long oval around Ethel Meyers and waited for the ghost to make her appearance.

We did not have to wait long. With a sudden shriek, Ethel, deep in trance, leapt to her feet, and in the awkward posture of an old crone, walked toward the front door. Nothing I could do would hold her back. I followed her quickly, as the medium, now possessed by the ghost, made her way through the long room to the door.

As if a strong wind had swept into the sitting room, the rest of the guests were thrown back by the sheer drive of Ethel's advance. She flung herself against the heavy wooden door and started to alternately gnaw at it and pound against it in an unmistakable desire to open it and go through. Then she seized the brass chain — the one Mrs. Witty had twice seen swinging by itself — and pulled it with astonishing force. I had all I could do to keep the medium from falling as she threw her body against the door.

In one hand I held a microphone, which I pressed close to her lips to catch as much of the dialogue as possible. I kept the other hand ready to prevent Ethel's fall to the floor.

"Rotten," the entranced medium now mumbled, still clutching the chain.

I tried to coax her back to the chair, but the ghost evidently would have none of it.

"It stinks . . . Where is it?"

"Is this your house?" I asked.

Heavy breathing.

"Yes. Get out!"

"I've come to help you. What is your name?"

"Get out!" the microphone picked up.

"What is it that you want?" I asked.

"My body."

"You've passed on, don't you understand?"

"No . . . I want my body. Where is it?"

I explained again that this was no longer her house, but she kept calling for the return of "her body" in such anger and despair that I began to wonder if it had not been buried on the premises.

"They took it, my body. I saw them, I saw them!"

"You must let go of this house. It is no longer yours," I said.

"No, my house, my house. They took it. My body. I have nothing. Get it. I feel I have one."

I explained that we had lent her a body to speak through for the moment.

"Who are you?" *It* sounded quieter.

"A friend," I replied, "come to help you."

Instead of replying, the entranced medium grabbed the door again.

"Why do you want to open the door?" I asked. It took a moment for the answer to come through trembling lips.

"Go out," she finally said. "I don't know you. Let me go, let me go."

I continued to question the ghost.

"Who are you? Did you live in this house?"

"My house. They took it out. My body is out there!"

I explained about the passage of time.

"You were not well. You've died."

"No, no . . . I wasn't cold."

"You are free to go from this door. Your loved ones, your family, await you outside."

"They hate me."

"No, they have made up with you. Why should they hate you?"

"They took me out the door."

Then, suddenly the medium's expression changed. Had someone come to fetch her?

"Oh, Baba, darling . . . Oh, he loved me."

There was hysterical crying now.

"He's gone . . . My beloved . . . "

"What is his name?"

"*Wain* . . . Where is he . . . Let me go!"

The crying was now almost uncontrollable, so I sent the ghost on her way. At the same time I asked that Albert, Ethel's control on the etheric side of the veil, take over her physical body for the moment to speak to us.

It took a moment or two until Albert was in command. The medium's body visibly straightened out and all traces of a bent old crone vanished. Albert's crisp voice was heard.

"She's a former tenant here, who has not been too well beloved. She also seems to have been carried out before complete death. This has brought her back to try and rectify it and make contact with the physical body. But here is always unhappiness. I believe there was no love toward her as she was older."

"Can you get a name?" I asked.

"If she refuses, I cannot."

"How long ago was this?"

"During the Nineties. Between 1890 and 1900."

"Is this a woman?"

"Yes."

"Anything peculiar about her appearance?"

"Large eyes, and almost a harelip."

"Why is she concerned about her body?"

"There was no great funeral for her. She was put in a box and a few words were said over her grave. That is part of her problem, that she was thus rejected and neglected."

"Why does she run up to the attic?"

"This was her house, and it was denied to her later in life."

"By whom?"

"By those living here. Relatives to her."

"Her heirs?"

"Those who took it over when she could no longer function. She was still alive."

"Anything else we should know?"

"There is a great deal of hate for anyone in this house. Her last days were full of hate. Should she return, if she is spoken to kindly, she will leave. We will help her."

"Why is she so full of hate?"

"Her grief, her oppressions. She never left her tongue quiet when she was disrupted in her desire to go from her quarters to the rest of the house."

"What was her character?"

"As a young person she was indeed a lady. Later in life, a strong personality, going slightly toward dual personality. She was an autocrat. At the very end, not beloved."

"And her relationship with the servants?"

"Not too friendly. Tyrannical."

"What troubled her about her servants?"

"They knew too much."

"Of what?"

"Her downfall. Her pride was hurt."

"Before that, how was she?"

"A suspicious woman. She could not help but take things from others which she believed were hers by right."

"What did she think her servants were doing?"

"They pried on her secret life. She trusted no one toward the end of life."

"Before she was prevented, as you say, from freely going about the house — did she have any belongings in the attic?"

"Yes, hidden. She trusted no one."

I then suggested that the "instrument" be brought back to herself. A very surprised Ethel Meyers awakened to find herself leaning against the entrance door.

"What's the matter with my lip?" she asked when she was able to speak. After a moment, Ethel Meyers was her old self, and the excursion into Mrs. Wainwright's world had come to an end.

The following morning Molly Smythe called me on the phone. "Remember about Albert's remarks that Mrs. Wainwright was restrained within her own rooms?"

Of course I remembered.

"Well," Molly continued, "we've just made a thorough investigation of all the doors upstairs in the servants' quarters where she spent her last years. They all show evidence of locks having been on them, later removed. *Someone was locked up there for sure.*"

Ironically, death had not released Mrs. Wainwright from confinement. To her, freedom still lay beyond the heavy wooden door with its brass chain.

Now that her spirit self had been taken in hand, perhaps she would find her way out of the maze of her delusions to rejoin her first husband, for whom she had called.

The next time Molly Smythe hears the front door opening, it'll be just her husband coming home from the office. *Or so I thought.*

But the last week of April, 1965, Molly called me again. Footsteps had been heard *upstairs* this time, and the sound of a door somewhere being opened and closed, and of course, on inspection, there was no one *visible* about.

Before I could make arrangements to come out to Rye once again, something else happened. Mr. Smythe was in the bathtub, when a large tube of toothpaste, safely resting well back on a shelf, flew off the shelf by its own volition. No vibration or other *natural* cause could account for it. Also, a hypodermic needle belonging to one of the nurses attending Molly's invalid mother had somehow disappeared.

I promised to bring Sybil Leek to the house. The British medium knew nothing whatever of the earlier history of the case, and I was curious to see if she would make contact with the same or different conditions, as sometimes happens when two mediums are used in the same house. It's like tuning in on different radio wavelengths.

It was a cool, wet day in May when we seated ourselves in a circle upstairs in the "haunted room." Present in addition to the hosts, Sybil Leek, and myself, were Mrs. Betty Salter (Molly's sister); David Ellingson, a reporter from the Port Chester, N.Y., *Item*; Mr. and Mrs. Robert Bendick, neighbors and friends of the Smythes; and Mary Melikian. Mr. Bendick was a television producer specializing in news programs.

Sybil went into hypnotic trance. It took several minutes before anything audible could be recorded.

"Who are you?" I asked.

A feeble voice answered:

"Marion . . . Marion Gernt . . . "

Before going into trance, Sybil had volunteered the information that the name "Grant," or something like it, had been on her mind ever since she set foot into the house.

"What year is this?" I asked.

"1706."

"Who built the house?"

"My father . . . Walden."

She then complained that people in the house were disturbing *her*, and that therefore she was *pulling it down*.

"My face is swollen," she added. "I'm sick . . . Blood."

Suddenly, something went wrong with my reliable tape recorder. In all my previous investigations it had worked perfectly. Now it wouldn't, and some parts of the conversation were not recorded. The wheels would turn and then stop, and then start again, as if someone were sticking their fingers into them at will!

I tried my camera, and to my amazement, I couldn't take any pictures. All of a sudden, the mechanism wouldn't function properly, and the shutter could not be un-cocked. I did not get any photographs. Bob Bendick, after the séance, took a good look at the camera. In a moment it was working fine again. After the séance, too, we tried to make the tape recorder work. It started and then stopped completely.

"The batteries have run out," I explained, confident that there was nothing more than that to it. So we put the machine on house current. Nothing happened. It wasn't the batteries. It was something else.

After we left the "haunted room" and went downstairs, I put the tape recorder into my traveling case. About ten minutes later, I heard a ghostly voice coming from my case. *My* voice. The tape recorder that I had left in a secure turn-off position had started up by itself . . . or . . . so it seemed.

But one can't be sure in haunted houses. *Item* reporter David Ellingson and Mary Melikian were standing next to me when it happened. John Smythe was wondering if someone had turned on the radio or TV. So much for the instruments that didn't work — temporarily.

But, let us get back to Sybil and the ghost speaking through her. She claimed to have been burned all over in a fire. John Smythe confirmed later that there were traces of a fire in the house that have never been satisfactorily explained.

The ghost seemed confused about it. She was burned, on this spot, in what was then a little house. The place was called Rocher. Her named was spelled M-a-r-i-o-n G-e-r-n-t. She was born at Rodey, eight miles distant. She was not sure about her age. At first she said 29, then it was 57. The house was built by one Dion, of Rocher.

I then tried to explain, as I always do, that the house belonged to someone else and that she must not stay.

"Go away," the ghost mumbled, not at all pleased with the idea of moving. But I insisted. I told her of her husband who wanted her to join him "over there."

"I hate him!" she volunteered, then added — "I start moving things . . . I break things up . . . I want my chair."

"You must not stay here," I pleaded. "You're not wanted here."

"*He* said that," she replied in a sullen voice. "Alfred did. My husband."

"You must join him and your children."

"I'll stay."

I repeated the incantation for her to leave.

"I can't go. I'm burned. I can't move," she countered.

I explained that these were only memories.

Finally she relented, and said — "I'll need a lot of rags . . . to cover myself."

Gently now, she started to fade.

"I need my chair," she pleaded, and I told her she could have it. Then she was gone.

Sybil came back now. Still in trance, she responded quickly to my questions about what she saw and felt on the other side of the veil. This is a technique I find particularly effective when used prior to bringing the medium out of trance or from under hypnosis.

"An old lady," Sybil said. "She is quite small. I think she is Dutch. Shriveled. She is very difficult. Can't move. Very unpleasant. Throws things because she can't walk. This is her house. She lived here about three hundred years ago. She wants everything *as it was*. She has marks on her face. She was in a fire."

"Did she die in it?" I asked.

"No. She died near here. Doesn't communicate well."

"There is a box with two hearts, two shields," Sybil said. "It means something to this woman."

"Were there any others around?" I asked.

"Lots, like shadows," Sybil explained, "but this little woman was the one causing the commotion."

"She likes to throw things," Sybil added, and I couldn't help thinking that she had never been briefed on all the objects the ghost had been throwing.

"She doesn't know where any doors are, so she just goes on. The door worries her a lot, because she doesn't know where it is. The front and rear have been changed around."

Sybil, of course, knew nothing of the noises centering around the main door, nor the fact that the rear of the house was once the front.

I told Sybil to send her away, and in a quiet voice, Sybil did so.

The séance was over, at least for the time being.

A little later, we went up to the top floor, where both Molly and

Sybil suddenly sensed a strong odor of perfume. I joined them, and I smelled it, too. It was as if *someone were following us about the house!*

But it was time to return to New York. Our hosts offered to drive us to the city.

"Too bad," I said in parting, "that nobody has *seen* an apparition here. Only sounds seem to have been noticed."

Betty Salter, Mrs. Smythe's perky sister, shook her head.

"Not true," she said. "I was here not so long ago when I saw a black figure downstairs in the dining room. I thought it was Molly, but on checking found that I was quite alone downstairs . . . That is, except for *her*."

Mrs. Wainwright, of course, was of Dutch ancestry, and the description of the character, appearance, and general impression of the ghost Sybil gave did rather fit Mrs. Wainwright.

Was the 1706 lady an ancestor or just someone who happened to be on the spot when only a small farm house occupied the site?

The Smythes really didn't care whether they have two ghosts or one ghost. They preferred to have none.

t Clock

ew England is full of ghosts.
ble first name of Dixie-Lee, and
ame of Danforth, lived in the
border in New Hampshire. She
dio program, and presto, there
mething pretty eerie that had

, she took on a two-week job as
e name of Mrs. William Collar.
een a fine artist, and had lived a
ee found being a companion an
Mrs. Collar's housekeeper went
anted someone with her in the
til she could find a full-time
would sleep in.

Collars had met in France, both studying there, and though
married against the wishes of their parents, they had a wonderful and happy life together. When Mr. William Collar died, things
were never the same. They had occupied a large double room on the
second floor, with a bed on either side, and a wash basin for each.
They truly lived close together.

After her husband's death, Mrs. Collar moved out of the room,
and never slept in it again. She left everything as it was, including a

big grandfather clock, which was never wound again after Mr. Collar's passing. Finally, in 1958, she joined her Bill. She may have been able to prepare herself for it, for she was often heard talking to "her Bill" when no one else could be seen in the room.

There was a fight over the will. The Collars had had no children, and a niece inherited the house.

But let me get back to Dixie-Lee and 1954. The young girl had moved into Mrs. Collar's imposing white house at New Ipswich, as the section was called, and given a room on the second floor next to the large bedroom once occupied by Mr. and Mrs. Collar. She had barely enough time to admire the expensive antique furniture around the house, when it was time to retire for the night.

Mrs. Dixie-Lee Danforth had come to Boston to meet me, and I questioned her about what happened then.

"I went to bed," she said, "and in the wee hours of the morning I awoke to the faint sound of footsteps and ticking of a clock. The sound of both kept getting louder — louder — till it seemed to beat against my brain."

At first she thought she was dreaming, but, biting her own hand, she realized she was fully awake. Cold sweat stood on her forehead when she realized that Mrs. Collar was an invalid *who could not walk*. What was more, the big clock had not worked for years. Suddenly, just as suddenly as it had come, it ceased. Dixie-Lee lay still for a while in sheer terror, then she turned on the light. Her bedroom door was firmly closed, just as she had left it before going to bed. She checked the door leading to what was once the Collars' big bedroom. It was shut tight, too. She ventured out onto the narrow landing of the staircase leading to the lower floor. It was shut off from the downstairs part of the house by a hall door. That, too, was shut. She retraced her steps and suddenly noticed a rope and pulley. She pulled it and another door appeared.

"I opened it, heart in my mouth," Dixie-Lee said, "and was

relieved to find a pretty, light bedroom behind it. It was furnished with modern furniture, and seemed to me much gayer and more peaceful than the rest of the house. The room was empty."

"What did you do then?" I wondered.

"First, I checked the big clock in my room. It was not going. Just as dead as it had been all those years. I looked around the house for other clocks. The only one in going condition was downstairs in the room occupied by Mrs. Collar, and I'd have to have had super-hearing to hear that one tick all the way up to the second floor through three sets of closed doors and a heavy wooden floor!"

I readily agreed that was not very likely, and wondered if she had told anyone of her frightening experience that night.

"I told the daytime housekeeper, with whom I was friendly, and she laughed. But I refused to stay another moment unless someone else stayed with me. She and her young daughter moved in with me upstairs, and stayed the full two weeks. I never heard the footsteps or the ticking of the clock again while they were with me. But after I left, housekeepers came and went. Nobody seemed to stay very long at the big white house in New Ipswich. Possibly they, too, heard the uncanny noises."

I nodded and asked about Mrs. Collar. Could she have gotten out of bed somehow?

"Not a chance," Dixie-Lee replied. "She was a total invalid. I checked on her in the morning. She had never left her bed. She couldn't have. Besides, the footsteps I heard weren't those of a frail old woman. *They were a man's heavy footfalls.* I never told Mrs. Collar about my experience though. Why frighten her to death?"

"Quite so," I agreed, and we talked about Dixie-Lee now. Was she psychic to any degree?

Dixie-Lee came from a most unusual family. Her great-grand-mother knew how 'to work the table.' Her grandfather saw the ghost of his sister, and Dixie-Lee herself had felt her late grandfather in his house whenever she visited, and she had numerous premonitions of impending danger.

On at least one such occasion she had a feeling she should not go on a certain trip, and insisted on stopping the car. On investigation, she found the wheels damaged. She might have been killed had she not heeded the warning!

We parted. Mrs. Danforth returned to her somewhat-more-than skeptical husband in Milford, and I took the next plane back to New York.

But the haunted house in New Ipswich never left my mind. I was due back in New England around Halloween, 1963, and decided to join Mrs. Danforth in a little trip up to the New Hampshire border country. A friend of hers, their children, a Boston-teacher friend of ours named Carol Bowman, and my wife and I completed the party that drove up to New Ipswich on that warm fall day. We weren't exactly expected, since I did not know the name of the present owner of the house. But Mrs. Danforth had sent word of our coming ahead. It turned out the word was never received, and we actually were lucky to find anyone in, luckier yet to be as cordially welcomed as we were by the lady of the house, whom we shall call Mrs. F.

Mrs. Jeanette F. was a sophisticated, well-educated lady whose husband was a psychiatrist, who was once also interested in parapsychology. She asked that I not use her full name here. A strange "feeling" of expecting us made her bid us a cordial welcome. I wasn't surprised to hear this — in this business, nothing surprises me anymore.

The F.'s had only had the house for a year when we visited them. They had not intended to buy the house, although they were on the lookout for a home in New England. But they passed it in their car, and fell in love with it . . . or rather were somehow made to buy the place. They discovered it was built in 1789. That wasn't all they discovered after they moved in.

"I always had the feeling," Mrs. F. said, "that we were only *allowed* to live here . . . but never really alone. Mrs. Collar's bedroom, for instance. I had the distinct feeling something was buried there under the floorboards. My sister-in-law slept upstairs. The next morning she told me she had 'heard things.' Right after we moved in, I heard footsteps upstairs."

"You too?" marveled Dixie-Lee, shooting a triumphant side glance at me, as if I had doubted her story.

"Last winter at dusk one day, I heard a woman scream. Both of us heard it, but we thought — or rather, *liked* to think — that it was a bobcat. Soon thereafter, we heard it again, only now it sounded more like a *child crying*. We heard it on several occasions and it gave us the willies."

On another occasion, there had been five people in the house when they heard the scream, followed by a growl. They went out to look for a bobcat . . . but there were absolutely no traces in the fresh snow, of either animal or human. There had also been all sorts of noises in the basement.

"Something strange about this child crying," Mrs. F. continued. "When we moved in, a neighbor came to see us and said when they saw we had a child, 'You've brought life back to the Collar house.'"

Dixie-Lee broke in.

"I seem to recall there was something about a child. I mean that they had a child."

"And it died?" I asked.

"I don't know," Mrs. F. said. "But there were diaries — they were almost lost, but one of Bill Collar's best friends, Archie Eaton, saved them. Here they are."

Mrs. F. showed us the remarkable books, all written in longhand. On cursory examination I did not uncover the secret of the child.

There is a hollow area in the basement. We went down to get "impressions," and Dixie-Lee felt very uneasy all of a sudden, and didn't feel like joining us downstairs, even though moments before she had been the spirit of adventure personified.

We returned to the ground floor and had some coffee.

I decided to return with a medium, and hold a séance next to the chimney down in the basement, underneath the room where Mrs. F. felt the floorboards held a secret.

But somehow we were thwarted in this effort.

In December of 1963, we were told that our visit would have to be postponed, and Mrs. F. asked us to come later in the winter. Too many living relatives in the house were making it difficult to listen for the dead.

"Something happened yesterday," she added, "that will interest you. My housekeeper is a very bright and trusted woman. She has never mentioned anything strange about the house. Yesterday I was telling her about our plans to sell the house. As I spoke, she was looking in the room next to me — I was standing in the kitchen. She was looking into the dining room, when she turned pale and interrupted me. She had seen a short, old woman in a long gray dress walk through the dining room. Now I questioned her about anything she might have seen in the past. She admitted she had seen figures on several occasions, but was afraid to be ridiculed. Strangely enough, she wants to buy the house despite these experiences. She calls it 'the house that watches,' because she always feels she is being observed while she cares for the children, even when she has them in the garden."

In February, 1964, we tried to fix a new date to visit the house. My letters remained unanswered. Had the house changed hands again?

But no matter who actually *lived* there. It seemed the *real* owner was still Mrs. Collar.

Hungry Lucy

"June Havoc's got a ghost in her townhouse," Gail Benedict said gaily on the telephone. Gail was in public relations, and a devoted ghost-finder ever since I had been able to rid her sister's apartment of a poltergeist the year before.

The house in question was 104 years old, stashed away in what New Yorkers called "Hell's Kitchen," the old area in the 40s between Ninth and Tenth Avenues, close to the theater district. Built on the corner of Forty-fourth Street and Ninth Avenue, it had been in the possession of the Rodenberg family until a Mr. Payne bought it. He remodeled it carefully, with a great deal of respect for the old plans. He did nothing to change its quaint Victorian appearance, inside or out.

About three years later, glamorous stage and television star June Havoc bought the house, and rented the upper floors to various tenants. She herself moved into the downstairs apartment, simply because no one else wanted it. It didn't strike her as strange at the time that no tenant had ever renewed the lease on that floor-through downstairs apartment, but now she knows why. It was all because of *Hungry Lucy*.

The morning after Gail's call, June Havoc telephoned me, and a séance was arranged for Friday of that week. I immediately reached British medium Sybil Leek, but I gave no details. I merely invited her to help me get rid of a noisy ghost. Noise was what June Havoc complained about.

"It seems to be a series of *insistent* sounds," she said. "First, they were rather soft. I didn't really notice them three years ago. Then I had the architect who built that balcony in the back come in and asked him to investigate these sounds. He said there was nothing whatever the matter with the house. Then I had the plumber up, because I thought it was the steam pipes. He said it was not that either. Then I had the carpenter in, for it is a very old house, but he couldn't find any structural defects whatever."

"When do you hear these tapping noises?"

"At all times. Lately, they seem to be more insistent. More demanding. We refer to it as 'tap dancing,' for that is exactly what it sounds like."

The wooden floors were in such excellent state that Miss Havoc didn't cover them with carpets. The yellow pine used for the floorboards cannot be replaced today.

June Havoc's maid had heard loud tapping in Miss Havoc's absence, and many of her actor friends had remarked on it.

"It is always in this area," June Havoc pointed out, "and seems to come from underneath the kitchen floor. It has become impossible to sleep a full night's sleep in this room."

The kitchen leads directly into the rear section of the floor-through apartment, to a room used as a bedroom. Consequently, any noise disturbed her sleep.

Underneath Miss Havoc's apartment, there was another floor-through, but the tenants had never reported anything unusual there, nor had the ones on the upper floors. Only Miss Havoc's place was noisy.

We now walked from the front of the apartment into the back half. Suddenly there was a loud tapping sound from underneath the floor, as if someone had shot off a machine gun. Catherine and I had arrived earlier than the rest, and there were just the three of us.

"There, you see," June Havoc said. The ghost had greeted us in style.

I stepped forward at once.

"What do you want?" I demanded.

Immediately, the noise stopped.

While we waited for the other participants in the investigation to arrive, June Havoc pointed to the rear wall.

"It has been furred out," she explained. "That is to say, there was another wall against the wall, which made the room smaller. Why, no one knows."

Soon *New York Post* columnist Earl Wilson and Mrs. Wilson, Gail Benedict, and Robert Winter-Berger, also a publicist, arrived, along with a woman from *Life* magazine, notebook in hand. A little later Sybil Leek swept into the room. There was a bit of casual conversation, in which nothing whatever was said about the ghost, and then we seated ourselves in the rear portion of the apartment. Sybil took the chair next to the spot where the noises always originated. June Havoc sat on her right, and I on her left. The lights were very bright since we were filming the entire scene for Miss Havoc's television show.

Soon enough, Sybil began to "go under."

"Hungry," Sybil mumbled faintly.

"Why are you hungry?" I asked.

"No food," the voice said.

The usually calm voice of Sybil Leek was panting in desperation now.

"I want some food, some food!" she cried.

I promised to help her and asked for her name.

"Don't cry. I will help you," I promised.

"Food . . . I want some food . . ." the voice continued to sob.

"Who are you?"

"Lucy Ryan."

"Do you live in this house?"

"No house here."

"How long have you been here?"

"A long time."

"What year is this?"

"Seventeen ninety-two."

"What do you do in this house?"

"No house . . . people . . . fields . . . "

"Why then are you here? What is there here for you?"

The ghost snorted.

"Hm . . . men."

"Who brought you here?"

"Came . . . people sent us away . . . soldiers . . . follow them . . . sent me away. . . ."

"What army? Which regiment?"

"Napier."

"How old are you?"

"Twenty."

"Where were you born?"

"Hawthorne . . . not very far away from here."

I was not sure whether she said "Hawthorne" or "Hawgton," or some similar name.

"What is your father's name?"

Silence.

"Your mother's name?"

Silence.

"Were you baptized?"

"Baptized?"

She didn't remember that either.

I explained that she had passed on. It did not matter.

"Stay here . . . until I get some food . . . meat . . . meat and corn . . . "

"Have you tried to communicate with anyone in this house?"

"Nobody listens."

"How are you trying to make them listen?"

"I make a noise because I want food."

"Why do you stay in one area? Why don't you move around freely?"

"Can't. Can't go away. Too many people. Soldiers."

"Where are your parents?"

"Dead."

"What is your mother's name?"

"Mae."

"Her maiden name?"

"Don't know."

"Your father's first name?"

"Terry."

"Were any of your family in the army?"

Ironical laughter punctuated her next words.

"Only . . . me."

"Tell me the names of some of the officers in the army you knew."

"Alfred . . . Wait."

"Any rank?"

"No rank."

"What regiment did you follow?"

"Just this . . . Alfred."

"And he left you?"

"Yes. I went with some other man, then I was hungry and I came here."

"Why here?"

"I was sent here."

"By whom?"

"They made me come. Picked me up. Man brought me here. Put me down on the ground."

"Did you die in this spot?"

"Die, die? I'm not dead. *I'm hungry.*"

I then asked her to join her parents, those who loved her, and to leave this spot. She refused. She wanted to walk by the river, she said. I suggested that she was not receiving food and could leave freely. After a while, the ghost seemed to slip away peacefully and Sybil Leek returned to her own body, temporarily vacated so that Lucy could speak through it. As usual, Sybil remembered absolutely nothing of what went on when she was in deep trance. She was crying, but thought her mascara was the cause of it.

Suddenly, the ghost was back. The floorboards were reverberating with the staccato sound of an angry tap, loud, strong, and demanding.

"What do you want?" I asked again, although I knew now what she wanted.

Sybil also extended a helping hand. But the sound stopped as abruptly as it had begun.

A while later, we sat down again. Sybil reported feeling two presences.

"One is a girl, the other is a man. A man with a stick. Or a gun. The girl is stronger. She wants something."

Suddenly, Sybil pointed to the kitchen area.

"What happened in the corner?"

Nobody had told Sybil of the area in which the disturbances had always taken place.

"I feel her behind me now. A youngish girl, not very well dressed, Georgian period. I don't get the man too well."

At this point, we brought into the room a small Victorian wooden table, a gift from Gail Benedict.

Within seconds after Sybil, June Havoc, and I had lightly placed our hands upon it, it started to move, seemingly of its own volition!

Rapidly, it began to tap out a word, using a kind of Morse code. While Earl Wilson was taking notes, we allowed the table to jump hither and yon, tapping out a message.

None of us touched the table top except lightly. There was no question of manipulating the table. The light was very bright, and our hands almost touched, so that any pressure by one of us would have been instantly noticed by the other two. This type of communication is slow, since the table runs through the entire alphabet until it reaches the desired letter, then the next letter, until an entire word has been spelled out.

"L-e-a-v-e," the communicator said, not exactly in a friendly mood.

Evidently she wanted the place to herself and thought *we* were the intruders.

I tried to get some more information about her. But instead of tapping out another word in an orderly fashion, the table became very excited — if that is the word for emotional tables — and practically leapt from beneath our hands. We were required to follow it to keep up the contact, as it careened wildly through the room. When I was speaking, it moved toward me and practically crept onto my lap. When I wasn't speaking, it ran to someone else in the room. Eventually, it became so wild, at times entirely off the floor, that it slipped from our light touch and, as the power was broken, instantly rolled into a corner — just another table with no life of its own.

We repaired to the garden, a few steps down an iron staircase, in the rear of the house.

"Sybil, what do you feel down here?" I asked.

"I had a tremendous urge to come out here. I didn't know there was a garden. Underneath my feet almost is the cause of the disturbance."

We were standing at a spot adjacent to the basement wall and close to the center of the tapping disturbance we had heard.

"Someone may be buried here," Sybil remarked, pointing to a mound of earth underneath our feet. "It's a girl."

"Do you see the wire covering the area behind you?" June Havoc said. "I tried to plant seeds there, and the wire was to protect them — but somehow nothing, nothing will grow there."

"Plant something on this mound," Sybil suggested. "It may well pacify *her*."

We returned to the upstairs apartment, and soon after broke up the "ghost hunting party," as columnist Sheila Graham called it later.

The next morning, I called June Havoc to see how things were. I knew from experience that the ghost would either be totally gone, or totally mad, but not the same as before.

Lucy, I was told, was rather mad. Twice as noisy, she still demanded her pound of flesh. I promised June Havoc that we'd return until the ghost was completely gone.

A few days passed. Things became a little quieter, as if Lucy were hesitating. Then something odd happened the next night. Instead of tapping from her accustomed corner area, Lucy moved away from it and tapped away from above June's bed. She had never been heard from that spot before.

I decided it was time to have a chat with Lucy again. Meanwhile, corroboration of the information we had obtained had come to us quickly. The morning after our first séance, Bob Winter-Berger called. He had been to the New York Public Library and checked on Napier, the officer named by the medium as the man in charge of the soldier's regiment.

The *Dictionary of National Biography* contained the answer. Colonel George Napier, a British officer, had served on the staff of Governor Sir Henry Clinton. How exciting, I thought. The Clinton mansion once occupied the very ground we were having the séance on. In fact, I had reported on a ghost at Clinton Court, two short blocks to the north, in *Ghost Hunter* and again in *Ghosts I've Met*. As far as I knew, the place was still not entirely free of the uncanny, for reports continued to reach me of strange steps and doors opening by themselves.

Although the mansion itself no longer stands, the carriage house in the rear was now part of Clinton Court, a reconstructed apartment house on West Forty-sixth Street. How could Sybil Leek, only recently arrived from England, have known of these things?

Napier was indeed the man who had charge of a regiment on this very spot, and the years 1781-1782 are given as the time when Napier's family contracted the dreaded yellow fever and died. Sir Henry Clinton forbade his aide to be in touch with them, and the Colonel was shipped off to England, half-dead himself, while his wife and family passed away on the spot that later became Potter's Field.

Many Irish immigrants came to the New World in those years. Perhaps the Ryan girl was one of them, or her parents were. Unfortunately, history does not keep much of a record of camp followers.

On January 15, 1965, precisely at midnight, I placed Sybil Leek into deep trance in my apartment on Riverside Drive. In the past we had succeeded in contacting *former* ghosts once they had been pried loose in an initial séance in the haunted house itself. I had high hopes that Lucy would communicate and I wasn't disappointed.

"Tick, tock, tickety-tock, June's clock stops, June's clock stops," the entranced medium murmured, barely audibly.

"Tickety-tock, June's clock stops, tickety-tock . . . "

"Who are you?" I asked.

"Lucy."

"Lucy, what does this mean?"

"June's clock stops, June's clock stops, frightened June, frightened June," she repeated like a child reciting a poem.

"Why do you want to frighten June?"

"Go away."

"Why do you want her to go away?"

"People there . . . too much house . . . too much June . . . too many clocks . . . she sings, she dances, she makes a lot of noise . . . I'm hungry, I'm always hungry. You don't do a thing about it . . . "

"Will you go away if I get you some food? Can we come to an agreement?"

"Why?"

"Because I want to help you, help June."

"Ah, same old story."

"You're not happy. Would you like to see Alfred again?"

"Yes . . . he's gone."

"Not very far. I'll get you together with Alfred if you will leave the house."

"Where would I go?"

"Alfred has a house of his own for you."

"Where?"

"Not very far."

"Frightened to go . . . don't know where to go . . . nobody likes me. She makes noises, I make noises. I don't like that clock."

"Where were you born, Lucy?"

"Larches by the Sea . . . Larchmont . . . by the Sea . . . people disturb me."

Again I asked her to go to join her Alfred, to find happiness again. I suggested she call for him by name, which she did, hesitatingly at first, more desperately later.

"No . . . I can't go from here. He said he would come. He said *wait*. Wait . . . here. Wait. Alfred, why don't you come? Too many clocks. Time, time, time . . . noisy creature. Time, time . . . three o'clock."

"What happened at three o'clock?" I demanded.

"He said he'd come," the ghost replied. "I waited for him."

"Why at three o'clock in the middle of the night?"

"Why do you think? Couldn't get out. Locked in. Not allowed out at night. I'll wait. He'll come."

"Did you meet any of his friends?"

"Not many . . . what would *I* say?"

"What was Alfred's name?"

"Bailey . . . Alfred said 'Wait, wait . . . I'll go away,' he said. 'They'll never find me.'"

"Go to him with my love," I said, calmly repeating over and over the formula used in rescue circle operations to send the earthbound ghost across the threshold.

As I spoke, Lucy slipped away from us, not violently as she had come, but more or less resignedly.

I telephoned June Havoc to see what had happened that night between midnight and 12:30. She had heard Lucy's tapping precisely then, but nothing more as the night passed — a quiet night for a change.

Was Lucy on her way to her Alfred?

We would know soon enough.

In the weeks that followed, I made periodic inquiries of June Havoc. Was the ghost still in evidence? Miss Havoc did not stay at her townhouse all the time, prefering the quiet charm of her Connecticut estate. But on the nights when she did sleep in the house on Forty-fourth Street, she was able to observe that Lucy Ryan had changed considerably in personality — the ghost had been freed, yes, but had not yet been driven from the house. In fact, the terrible noise was now all over the house, although less frequent and less vehement — *as if she were thinking things over.*

I decided we had to finish the job as well as we could and another séance was arranged for late March, 1965. Present were — in addition to our hostess and chief sufferer — my wife Catherine and myself; Emory Lewis, editor of *Cue* magazine; Barry Farber, WOR commentator; and two friends of June Havoc. We grouped ourselves around a table in the *front room* this time. This soon proved to be a mistake. No Lucy Ryan. No ghost. We repaired to the other room where the original manifestations had taken place, with more luck this time.

Sybil, in trance, told us that the girl had gone, but that Alfred had no intention of leaving. He was waiting for *her* now. I asked for the name of his commanding officer and was told it was Napier. This we knew already. But who was the next in rank?

"Lieutenant William Watkins."

"What about the commanding general?"

He did not know.

He had been born in Hawthorne, just like Lucy, he told Sybil. I had been able to trace this Hawthorne to a place not far away in Westchester County.

There were people all over, Sybil said in trance, and they were falling down. They were ill.

"Send Alfred to join his Lucy," I commanded, and Sybil in a low voice told the stubborn ghost to go.

After an interlude of table tipping, in which several characters from the nether world made their auditory appearance, she returned to trance. Sybil in trance was near the river again, among the sick.

But no Lucy Ryan. Lucy's gone, she said.

"The smell makes me sick," Sybil said, and you could see stark horror in her sensitive face.

"Dirty people, rags, people in uniform too, with dirty trousers. There is a big house across the river."

"Whose house is it?"

"Mr. Dawson's. Doctor Dawson. Dr. James Dawson . . . Lee Point. Must go there. Feel sick. Rocks and trees, just the house across the river."

"What year is this?"

"Ninety-two."

She then described Dr. Dawson's house as having three windows on the left, two on the right, and five above, and said that it was called Lee Point — Hawthorne. It sounded a little like Hawgton to me, but I can't be sure.

Over the river, she said. She described a "round thing on a post" in front of the house, like a shell. For messages, she thought.

"What is the name of the country we're in?" I asked.

"Vinelands. Vinelands."

I decided to change the subject back to Hungry Lucy. How did she get sick?

"She didn't get any food, and then she got cold, by the river.

". . . Nobody helped them here. Let them die. Buried them in a pit."

"What is the name of the river?"

"Mo . . . Mo-something."

"Do you see anyone else still around?"

"Lots of people with black faces, black shapes."

The plague, I thought, and how little the doctors could do in those days to stem it.

I asked about the man in charge and she said "Napier" and I wondered who would be left in command after Napier left, and the answer this time was, "Clinton . . . old fool. Georgie."

There were a Henry Clinton and a George Clinton, fairly contemporary with each other.

"What happened after that?"

"Napier died."

"Any other officers around?"

"Little Boy Richardson . . . Lieutenant."

"What regiment?"

"Burgoyne."

Sybil, entranced, started to hiss and whistle. "Signals," she murmured. "As the men go away, they whistle."

I decided the time had come to bring Sybil out of trance. She felt none the worse for it, and asked for something to drink. *Hungry*, like Lucy, she wasn't.

We began to evaluate the information just obtained. Dr. James

Dawson may very well have lived. The A.M.A. membership directories aren't that old. I found the mention of Lee Point and Hawthorne interesting, inasmuch as the two locations are quite close. Lee, of course, would be Fort Lee, and there is a "point" or promontory in the river at that spot.

The town of Vinelands does exist in New Jersey, but the river beginning with "Mo-" may be the Mohawk. That Burgoyne was a general in the British army during the Revolution is well known.

So there you have it. Sybil Leek knows very little, if anything, about the New Jersey and Westchester countryside, having only recently come to America. Even I, then a New York resident for 27 years, had never heard of Hawthorne before. Yet there it is on the way to Pleasantville, New York.

The proof of the ghostly pudding, however, was not the regimental roster, but the state of affairs at June Havoc's house.

A later report had it that Lucy, Alfred, or whoever was responsible, had quieted down considerably.

They were down, but not out.

I tactfully explained to June Havoc that feeling sorry for a hungry ghost makes things tough for a parapsychologist. The emotional pull of a genuine attachment, no matter how unconscious it may be, can provide the energies necessary to prolong the stay of the ghost.

Gradually, as June Havoc — wanting a peaceful house, especially at 3 A.M. — allowed practical sense to outweigh sentimentality, the shades of Hungry Lucy and her soldier-boy faded into the distant past, whence they came.

Proper Bostonian Ghosts

The proper Bostonian ghosts here are not the political skeletons rattling in many a Back Bay closet. In Boston, a ghost is a ghost. But make no mistake, something of their English forebears has rubbed off on many a Bostonian. They take their specters with grim pride and a matter of nature — it is part of the regional scenery, so to speak, and really all terribly chic, but the Bostonian prefers to pretend it's nothing much. Far from it. New England ghosts can be pretty exciting stuff.

Sometimes New Englanders take the memories of their ghosts with them even when they move to other states. A Mrs. C. E. Foster once wrote me from Indianapolis about her grandmother, who seems to have been buried alive. At the time her grandmother, Louisa Wallace, was lowered into her grave in Revere, Massachusetts, Mrs. Foster had a vision of her in the casket . . . and heard her cough. The dead don't do that, and Mrs. Foster thinks her grandmother tried to tell her that she wasn't quite ready yet. Unfortunately, nothing was done about it at the time, so she went, ready or not.

. . . .

Many of my contacts have been made through a Boston radio program called "Contact," with Bob Kennedy, on Station WBZ. I appeared on it many times and always found it most rewarding. After one of my radio stints in the fall of 1963, I was approached by a young lady with the appealing name of Aimee Violante, a nurse who had a most interesting and rather touching experience she wanted to tell me about.

"In 1957, my boyfriend took me to Lake Quannapowette outside of Boston. We rented a rowboat and rowed to the other side of the lake to go swimming, as swimming was prohibited there.

"In the boat, I sat facing the opposite shore. We were heading for a strip of beach with a few benches on it. There were three benches. It was nearing dusk. Sitting on these benches were elderly people all dressed in white. The ladies were dressed in silky dresses, wearing big picture hats and gloves. The men wore white suits. They were just sitting watching us. They weren't frightening, so I didn't pay too much attention to them, but I was angry that my boyfriend was pulling in there, as I thought they would say something about us going swimming. He didn't see them, as his back was toward them, and when we pulled up, they were gone.

"When we rowed back, I was wondering where they all went to, so I asked him. When I told him about the people I saw, he got frightened and hurried me back to the car. There he told me that on the side we were on was a cemetery, and there was no way any people could get to the benches once the gates were closed."

....

The Peter Hofmann family consisted of husband, wife Pennie, and baby — then about three or four years old. The parents were articulate, well-educated people making their home in Harvard. Not Harvard University, but Harvard near Ayer, Massachusetts, about an hour's ride from the university.

An automobile accident in 1956 had left Mrs. Hofmann partially paralyzed, but her keen gift of observation was not impaired. She had always had a peculiar liking for graveyards, and her first psychic experience, in 1951, consisted of a vision of a horse-drawn hearse that had passed near a cemetery. One could argue that lots of such hearses used to pull into cemeteries, but the fact remains that Mrs. Hofmann's was not a real one.

Their house stands next to a house built by Mrs. Hofmann's father, a well-known physician, and it seemed that both houses were haunted. The larger house, owned by Mrs. Hofmann's father, was built in 1721 "on the bounty received from an Indian scalp."

From the first moment she saw it, Pennie Hofmann had odd sensations about it. In 1960 or 1961, she and her husband were spending the night there, when at about two in the morning they both woke up for no apparent reason.

"I spoke to what I thought was Pete," she said, "as I could see someone by the front window, but it turned out that Pete was *behind* me. Needless to say, we left right away."

Peter Hofmann nodded and added: "I myself have been in the house at night a few times alone, and I've always had the feeling I was being watched."

Then in late October, 1963, Pennie Hofmann phoned me in New York. Could I please come to Boston and tell her if she was *seeing things?*

What sort of things, I asked.

"Well," she replied, somewhat upset, "we'd been staying over in my father's house again a week ago. I saw a soldier in the bedroom. He was dark and had a noose around the neck; the rope was cut and his face seemed almost luminous. I swear I saw him."

I hurried to Boston and they met me at radio station WBZ.

What about the ghostly soldier? Any clues?

Both Hofmanns nodded.

"We've checked in Nourse's *History of the Town of Harvard,*" Mrs. Hoffman said gravely, "and there was a Colonial drummer named Hill who was hanged in this area . . . for some misdeeds."

I remembered her telling me of a ghost in their own house on Poor Farm Road, and Mrs. Hofmann filled me in on this far gentler wraith.

"During the summer months, " she explained, "there is what appears to be a Quaker lady that walks across our front lawn, usually during the afternoon. This person often appears many times a day."

Her husband added that she had given him many details of the ghost's dress, which he checked for authenticity. He found that they were indeed worn by the Quaker women of the eighteenth century.

Why a member of so gentle a persuasion as the Quakers would turn into a ghost we may never know, but perhaps someday the Quaker lady will walk again for me.

....

There is said to be the ghost of a pirate near the water's edge in old Boston, where so many secret passages existed in the days when Massachusetts was British. The *Black Lady of Warren Island,* out in the bay, has been seen by a number of people. She was executed during the Civil War for helping her husband, a Yankee prisoner, break out of prison.

Boston's emotional climate is fine for special activities. There may not be any medieval castles, but Beacon Hill can look pretty forbidding, too — especially on a chilly November night when the fog drifts in from the sea.

In September of 1963 I appeared on WBZ-TV on Mike Douglas's television show, discussing my ever-present interest in haunted houses. As a consequence, there was an avalanche of letters, many of which contained leads to new cases.

One came from a Mrs. Anne Valukis, of South Natick, near Boston, Massachusetts. She wrote me of an old house she lived in where the stairs creaked unaccountably at odd times, as if someone were walking up and down them; of the strange behavior her little boy showed whenever he was in a certain room of the house; and of an overall atmosphere of the uncanny prevailing throughout the house, as if an unseen force were always present.

I wrote for additional data about herself and the background of the house. Meanwhile, the public television station in Boston, Channel 2, took an interest in my work, and the station and I decided to join forces for an expedition to the haunted house in South Natick. Fred Barzyk, the director, undertook the preliminary task of additional research. My visit was scheduled for the last week of October. Mrs. Valukis wasn't long in answering me.

"The stairs haven't creaked for over a week, but my four year old woke Saturday night four times, and was really scared, so much so he would not go back upstairs to his room . . . Years ago this house was kind of a speakeasy, connected to a dance hall that was on the Charles River. Probably anything could have happened here. Who knows?"

Not because of the spooky stairs, but for other reasons, the Valukis family decided to move to Anne's parents' house. This made our visit problematical, until Fred Barzyk discovered that the house belonging to Mrs. Valukis' parents was even more haunted than Anne Valukis' place.

Mrs. Rose Josselyn, Anne's mother, was a Canadian Indian, and, like many of her people, had had psychic experiences all her life.

About 39 years before I met her, Mrs. Josselyn was living in Annapolis Royal, Canada, in what was purported to be a haunted house. Frequently she awoke in the middle of the night and found it difficult to breathe. Her arms seemed to be pinned down by an unseen force and she was unable to move even so much as a finger!

"It felt as if someone were choking me," she said to me later. "I tried to scream, but could not move my lips."

This had gone on for about a year. Finally Rose told her mother, who was mediumistic herself, and Rose was forbidden ever to sleep again in "that room." Twenty years later, Mrs. Josselyn still remembered the stark terror of those nights in Canada, but nothing like it had happened to her since — nothing, that is, until she moved into this house.

The house itself was a gray-white, medium-sized early American house, built in the stately manner of early Georgian architecture and very well preserved. It was set back from the road a bit, framed by tall, shady trees, and one had the feeling of being far from the bustle of the big city. Built about 150 years before, the house had an upper story and a total of eight rooms. Bordering on the lawn of the house was a cemetery, separated from the Josselyn house by an iron gate and fence.

When the Josselyns moved in with their family, Mrs. Josselyn had no thoughts of anything psychic or uncanny. She soon learned differently.

Upstairs, there were two bedrooms separated only by a thin wall. The larger one belonged to Mrs. Josselyn; the smaller one, to the rear of the house, to her husband Roy. It was in her bedroom that Mrs. Josselyn had another attack of the terrible feeling she had experienced in her Canadian youth. Pinned down on her bed, it was as if someone were upon her, holding her.

"Whose bedroom was this before you took it?" I inquired.

"Well, my daughter-in-law slept here for awhile," Mrs. Josselyn confided, "that is, before she died."

I asked further questions about this girl. At the age of 21, she had fallen ill and suffered her last agonies in this very room, before being taken off to a hospital, never to return. Her only child, to whom she was naturally very attached, was reared by Mrs. Josselyn and Mrs. Valukis.

I walked across the floor to a small room belonging to David Josselyn, 17, the brother of Mrs. Valukis. Here I was shown a hand-made wooden chair that was said to creak at odd moments, as if someone were sitting in it. David himself had been awakened many times by this unearthly behavior of his chair, and Anne had also observed the noise. I tried the chair. It was sturdy enough, and only strong efforts on my part produced any kind of noise. It could not have creaked by itself.

"Who gave you this chair?" I asked.

"The same man who made our clock downstairs," David said. I recalled seeing a beautiful wooden grandfather clock in the corner of the downstairs room. The odd thing about that clock was it sometimes ticked and the hands moved, even though it no longer had any works or pendulum!

The clock, chair, and a desk in David's room were the work of a skilled craftsman named Thomas Council, who was a well-liked house guest of the Josselyns and gave them these things to show his gratitude for their hospitality. He was a lonely bachelor and the Josselyns were his only close friends. David in particular was the apple of his eye. Thomas Council's body rested comfortably, it is hoped, across the way in the cemetery, and the Josselyns made sure there were always fresh flowers on his grave.

I decided to return to Mrs. Josselyn's room.

"Outside of your nightmarish experiences here and in Canada," I said, "have you had any other psychic incidents?"

Mrs. Josselyn, a serious, quiet woman of about 59, thought for a moment.

"Yes, frequently. Whenever my children are in some sort of trouble, I just know it. No matter how trifling. You might say we have telepathic contact."

"Did you also hear those stairs creak at your daughter's house across the road?"

"Yes, many times."

"Was that after or before your daughter-in-law passed away?"

"After."

"I clearly heard those steps upstairs, and there wasn't anyone but me and the baby in the house," added Anne Valukis for corroboration.

They all had been visited, it seemed to me, except the father, Roy Josselyn. It was time I turned my attention in his direction.

Mr. Josselyn sat on the bed in his room, quietly smoking a pipe. I had been warned by Fred Barzyk that the man of the house was no particular believer in the supernatural. To my relief, I discovered Mr. Josselyn at least had an open mind. I also discovered that a great-aunt of his in Vermont had been a spiritualistic medium.

I asked if he had seen or heard anything unusual.

"Well," he said, "about a year ago I started to hear some moans and groans around here . . . " he pointed toward the wall adjoining the bedroom occupied by his wife. "At first I thought it was my wife, but there was no one in her room at the time. I looked."

"This moaning . . . was it a human voice?"

"Oh yes, very human. Couldn't sleep a wink while it lasted."

"When did you last hear it?"

"Yesterday," he said laconically.

"How did you and your daughter-in-law get along?" I suddenly felt compelled to ask.

"Very well," he said. "As a matter of fact, she took more to me than to anyone else. You know how women are — a bit jealous. She was a little on the possessive side as far as her baby was concerned. I mean, she was very much worried about the child."

"But she wasn't jealous of you?"

"No, not of me. We were very close."

I thought of the 21-year-old girl taken by death without being ready for it, and the thoughts of fear for her child that must have gone through her mind those dreadful last hours when her moaning filled the air of the room next to Roy Josselyn's.

I also thought about Mrs. Roy Josselyn's background — the fact that she was Princess of the Micmac Indian Tribe. I remembered how frequent psychic experiences were among Indians, who are so much closer to nature than we city-dwellers.

Perhaps the restless spirit of the 21-year-old girl wanted some attention. Perhaps her final moments had only impressed themselves on the atmosphere of the upstairs room and were relived by the psychically sensitive members of the family. Perhaps, too, Thomas Council, the family friend, roamed the house now and then to make sure everything was all right with his favorite family.

When we drove back to Boston late that night, I felt sure I had met a haunted family, for better or worse.

The Ghost of Gay Street

*F*rank Paris and T. E. Lewis were puppeteers. Children came to admire the little theater the two puppeteers had set up in the high-ceilinged basement of their old house in Greenwich Village, that old section of New York going back to the 1700s. The house at number 12 Gay Street was a typical old townhouse, smallish, the kind New Yorkers built around 1800 when "the village" meant *far uptown*.

In 1924, a second section was added to the house, covering the garden that used to grace the back of the house. This architectural graft created a kind of duplex, one apartment on top of another, with small rooms at the sides in the rear.

The ownership of the house in the early days is hazy. At one time a sculptor owned number 12, possibly before the 1930s. Evidently he was fond of bootleg liquor, for he built a trap door in the ground floor of the newer section of the house, probably over his hidden liquor cabinet. Before that, Mayor Jimmy Walker owned the house, and used it *well*, although not *wisely*. One of his many loves is said to have been the tenant there. By a strange set of circumstances, the records of the house vanished like a ghost from the files of the Hall of Records around that time.

Later, real-estate broker Mary Ellen Strunsky lived in the house. In 1956, she sold it to the puppeteer team of Paris and Lewis, who had been there ever since, living in the upstairs apartment and using the lower portion as a workroom and studio for their little theater.

None of this, incidentally, was known to me until after the visit I paid the house in the company of my medium for the evening, Betty Ritter.

It all started when a reporter from the *New York World-Telegram*, Cindy Hughes, came to interview me, and casually dropped a hint that she knew of a haunted house. Faster than you can say *Journal-American*, I had her promise to lead me to this house. On a particularly warm night in May of 1963, I followed Miss Hughes down to Gay Street. Betty Ritter knew nothing at all about the case; she didn't even know the address where we were going.

We were greeted warmly by Frank Paris, who led us up the stairs into the upper apartment. The sight of the elaborately furnished, huge living room was surprising. Oriental figurines, heavy drapes, paintings, statuary, and antiques filled the room.

In two comfortable chairs we found awaiting us two friends of the owners: an intense looking man in his thirties, Richard X., who, I later discovered, was an editor by profession, and Alice May Hall, a charming lady of undetermined age.

I managed to get Betty out of earshot, so I could question these people without her getting impressions from our conversation.

"What is this about the house being haunted?" I asked Frank Paris.

He nodded gravely.

"I was working downstairs with some lacquer. It was late, around 3 A.M. Suddenly, I began to smell a strong odor of violets. My black spaniel here also smelled it, for he started to sniff rather strangely. And yet, Ted, my partner, in the same room with me, did not get the strange scent at all. But there is more. People waltz up and down the stairs at night, time and again."

"What do you mean, *waltz?*"

"I mean they go up and down, up and down, as if they had business here," Frank explained, and I thought, perhaps they had, perhaps they had.

"A weekend visitor also had a most peculiar experience here," Frank Paris continued. "He knew nothing about our haunted reputation, of course. We were away on a short trip, and when we got back, he greeted us with — 'Say, who are all these people going up and down the stairs?' He had thought that the house next door was somehow connected to ours, and that what he heard were people from next door. But of course, there is no connection whatever."

"And did you ever investigate these mysterious footsteps?" I asked.

"Many times," Frank and Ted nodded simultaneously, "but there was never anyone there — anyone of flesh-and-blood, that is."

I thanked them, and wondered aloud if they weren't psychic, since they had experienced what can only be called psychic phenomena.

Frank Paris hesitated, then admitted that he thought both of them were to some extent.

"We had a little dog which we had to have put away one day. We loved the dog very much, but it was one of those things that had to be done. For over a year after the dog's death, both of us felt him poking us in the leg — a habit he had in life. This happened on many occasions to both of us."

I walked over to where Miss Hall, the gray-haired little lady, sat.

"Oh, there is a ghost here all right," she volunteered. "It was in February of 1963, and I happened to be in the house, since the boys and I are good friends. I was sitting here in this very spot, relaxing and casually looking toward the entrance door through which you just came — the one that leads to the hallway and the stairs. There was a man there, wearing evening clothes, and an Inverness Cape —

I saw him quite plainly. He had dark hair. It was dusk, and there was still some light outside."

"What did you do?"

"I turned my head to tell Frank Paris about the stranger, and that instant he was gone like a puff of smoke."

Paris broke in.

"I questioned her about this, since I didn't really believe it. But a week later, at dawn this time, I saw the ghost myself, exactly as Alice had described him — wearing evening clothes, a cape, hat, and his face somewhat obscured by the shadows of the hallway. Both Alice and I are sure he was a youngish man, and had sparkling eyes. What's more, our dog also saw the intruder. He went up to the ghost, friendly-like, as if to greet him."

Those were the facts of the case. A ghost in evening clothes, an old house where heaven knows what might have happened at one time or another, and a handful of psychic people.

I returned to Betty Ritter, and asked her to gather psychic impressions while walking about the house.

"A crime was committed here," the medium said, and described a terrible argument upstairs between an Oriental and a woman. She described a gambling den, opium smokers, and a language she could not understand. The man's name was Ming, she said. Ming is a very common Chinese word meaning, I believe, Sun.

Betty also told Frank Paris that someone close to him by the name of John had passed on and that he had something wrong with his right eye, which Paris acknowledged was correct. She told Ted Lewis that a Bernard L. was around him, not knowing, of course, that Lewis' father was named Bernham Lewis. She told Richard X. that he worked with books, and it was not until after the séance that I learned he was an editor by profession. I don't know about the Chinese and the opium den, but they are possibilities in an area so far removed from the bright lights of the city as the Village once was.

We went downstairs and, in the almost total darkness, formed a circle. Betty fell into trance, her neck suddenly falling back as if she were being possessed by a woman whose neck had been hurt.

"Emil," she mumbled, and added the woman had been decapitated, and her bones were still about. She then came out of trance and we walked back up the stairs to the oldest part of the house. Still "seeing" clairvoyantly, Betty Ritter again mumbled "Emil," and said she saw documents with government seals on them. She also felt someone named Mary Ellen had lived here and earlier some "well-known government official named Wilkins or Wilkinson."

Betty, of course, knew nothing about real-estate broker Mary Ellen Strunsky or Jimmy Walker, the former New York Mayor, who had been in this house for so long.

It now remained for us to find those bones Betty had talked about. We returned to the downstairs portion of the house, but Betty refused to go farther. Her impression of tragedy was so strong she urged us to desist.

Thus it was that the Ghost of Gay Street, whoever he may be, would have to wait just a little longer until the bones could be properly sorted out. It wasn't half bad, considering that Frank Paris and Ted Lewis put on a pretty nice puppet show every so often, down there in the murky basement theater at number 12 Gay Street.

When The Dead Stay On

Nothing is so exasperating as a dead person in a living household. I mean a ghost has a way of disturbing things far beyond the powers held by the wraith while still among the quick. Very few people realize that a ghost is not someone out to pester you for the sake of being an annoyance, or to attract attention for the sake of being difficult. Far from it. We know by now that ghosts are unhappy beings caught between two states and unable to adjust to either one.

Most people "pass over" without difficulty and are rarely heard from again, except when a spiritualist insists on raising them, or when an emergency occurs among the family that makes intervention by the departed a desired, or even necessary, matter.

They do their bit, and then go again, looking back at their handiwork with justified pride. *The dead are always among us,* make no mistake about that. They obey their own set of laws that forbids them to approach us or let us know their presence except when conditions require it. But they can do other things to let us feel them near, and these little things can mean a great deal when they are recognized as sure signs of a loved one's nearness.

Tragedies create ghosts through shock conditions, and nothing can send them out of the place where they found a sad end except the realization of their own emotional entanglement. This can be accomplished by allowing them to communicate through trance. But there are also cases in which the tragedy is not sudden, but gradual, and the unnatural attachment to physical life creates the ghost syndrome. The person who refuses to accept peacefully the transition called death, and holds on to material surroundings, becomes a ghost when these feelings of resistance and attachment become psychotic.

Such persons will then regard the houses they lived and died in as still theirs, and will look on later owners or tenants as merely unwanted intruders who must be forced out of the place by any means available. The natural way to accomplish this is to show themselves to the living as often as possible, to assert their continued ownership. If that won't do it, move objects, throw things, make noises — let them know whose house this is!

The reports of such happenings are many. Every week brings new cases from reliable and verified witnesses, and the pattern begins to emerge pretty clearly.

A lady from Ridgewood, New York, wrote to me about a certain house on Division Avenue in Brooklyn, where she had lived as a child. A young grandmother, Mrs. Petre had a good education and an equally good memory. She remembered the name of her landlord while she was still a youngster, and even the names of *all* her teachers at Public School 19. The house her family had rented consisted of a basement, parlor floor, and a top floor where the bedrooms were located.

On a certain warm October day, she found herself in the basement, while her mother was upstairs. She knew there was no one else in the house. When she glanced at the glass door shutting off the stairs, with the glass pane acting almost like a mirror, she saw to her amazement a man peeking around the doorway. Moments before she had heard heavy footsteps coming down the stairs, and wondered if someone had gotten into the house while she and her mother had been out shopping. She screamed and ran out of the house, but did not tell her family about the stranger.

Sometime after, she sat facing the same stairs in the company of her brother and sister-in-law, when she heard the footsteps again and the stranger appeared. Only this time she got a good look at him and was able to describe his thin, very pale face, his black hair, and the black suit and fedora hat he wore.

Nobody believed the girl, of course, and even the landlady accused her of imagining all this. But after a year, her father became alarmed at his daughter's nervousness and decided to move. Finally, the landlady asked for details of the apparition, and listened as the girl described the ghost she had seen.

"My God," the landlady, a Mrs. Grimshaw, finally said. "I knew that man — he hanged himself on the top floor!"

....

Sometimes the dead will only stay on until things have been straightened out to their taste. Anna Arrington was a lady with the gift of mediumship who lived in New York State. In 1944, her mother-in-law, a woman of some wealth, passed on in Wilmington, North Carolina, and was buried there. There was some question about her will. Three days after her death, Mrs. Arrington was awakened from heavy sleep at 3 A.M. by a hand touching hers.

Her first thought was that one of her two children wanted something. On awakening, however, she saw her mother-in-law in a flowing white gown standing at the foot of her bed. While her husband continued to snore, the ghost put a finger to Mrs. Arrington's lips and asked her not to awaken her son, but to remember that the missing will was in the dining room of her house on top of the dish closet under a sugar bowl. Mrs. Arrington was roundly laughed at by her husband the next morning, but several days later his sister returned from Wilmington (the Arringtons lived in New York City at the time) and confirmed that the will had indeed been found where the ghost had indicated.

....

Back in the 1960s, I was approached by a gentleman named Paul Herring, who was born in Germany, and who lived in a small apartment on Manhattan's Eastside as well as in a country house in Westchester County, New York. He was in the restaurant business and not given to dreaming or speculation. He struck me as a simple, solid citizen. His aged mother, also German-born, lived with him, and a large German shepherd dog completed the household.

Mr. Herring was not married, and his mother was a widow. What caused them to reach me was the peculiar way in which steps were heard around the Westchester house when nobody was walking. On three separate occasions, Mrs. Herring saw an apparition in her living room.

"It was sort of blackish," she said, "but I recognized it instantly. It was my late husband."

The "black outline" of a man also appeared near light fixtures, and there were noises in the house that had no natural origins.

"The doors are forever opening and closing by themselves," the son added. "We're going crazy trying to keep up with that spook."

Their bedspreads were being pulled off at night. They were touched on the face by an unseen hand, especially after dark.

The September before, Mrs. Herring was approaching the swinging doors of the living room, when the door moved out by itself and met her! A table in the kitchen moved by its own volition in plain daylight.

Her other son, Max, who lived in Norfolk, Virginia, always left the house in a hurry because "he can't breathe" in it. Her dog, Noxy, was forever disturbed when they were out in the Westchester house.

"How long has this been going on, Mrs. Herring?" I asked.

"About four years at least," the spunky lady replied, "but my husband died ten years ago."

It then developed that he had divorced her and married another woman, and there were no surviving children from that union. Still, the "other woman" had kept all of Mr. Herring Sr.'s money — no valid will was ever found. Was the ghost protesting this injustice to his companion of so many years? Was he regretting his hasty step divorcing her and marrying another?

The Herrings weren't the only ones to hear the footsteps. A prospective tenant who came to rent the country house fled after hearing someone walk *through a closed door.*

....

Mrs. E. F. Newbold seems to have been followed by ghosts since childhood — as if she were carrying a lamp aloft to let the denizens of the nether world know she had the sixth sense.

"I'm haunted," she said. "I've been followed by a 'what's it' since I was quite young. It simply pulls the back of my skirt. No more than that, but when you're alone in the middle of a room, this can be awfully disconcerting."

I thought of Grandma Thurston's ghost, and how she had pulled my elbow a couple of years before while I was investigating an empty room in a pre-Colonial house in Connecticut, and I couldn't agree more. Mrs. Newbold's family had psychic experiences also. Her little girl had felt a hand on her shoulder. It ran in the family.

"My husband's aunt died in Florida, while I was in New Jersey. We had been very close, and I said good-bye to her body here at the funeral at 10 A.M. At 9 P.M. I went into my kitchen and though I could not see her, I *knew* she was sitting at the table, staring at my back, and pleading with me."

"What about this skirt pulling?"

"It has followed me through a house, an apartment, a succession of rented rooms, two new houses, and two old houses. I've had a feeling of not being alone, and of sadness. I've also felt a hand on my shoulder, and heard pacing footsteps, always overhead.

"The next house we lived in was about 35 years old, had had only one owner, still alive, and no one had died there. It looked like a haunted house, but it was only from neglect. We modernized it, and *then* it started! Pulling at my skirt went on fairly often. One night when I was alone, that is, my husband was out of town and our three children were sound asleep — I checked them just before and just after — I was watching TV in the living room, when I heard the outside cellar door open. I looked out the window to see if someone was breaking in, since I had locked the door shortly before. While I was watching, I *heard* it close firmly. The door didn't move, however. This door had a distinctive sound so I couldn't have mistaken it.

"I went back to my seat and picked up my scissors, wishing for a gun. I was sure I heard a prowler. Now I heard slow footsteps come up from the cellar, through the laundry room, kitchen, into the living room, right past me, and up the stairs to the second floor. They stopped at the top of the stairs, and I never heard it again. Nor do I want to. Those steps went past me, no more than five feet away, and the room was empty. Unfortunately, I have no corroboration, but I *was* wide awake and perfectly sober!"

So much for the lady from Harrington Park, New Jersey.

....

Miss Margaret C. and her family lived in what surely was a haunted house, so that I won't give her full name. But here is her report.

"In December of 1955, just two days before Christmas, I traveled to Pennsylvania to spend the holidays with my sister and her husband. They lived on the second floor (the apartment I am now renting) of a spacious mid-Victorian-style home built around a hundred years ago.

"Due to the death of my sister's mother-in-law, who had resided on the first floor of the house, the occasion was not an entirely joyous one, but we came for the sake of my brother-in-law.

"Having come all the way from Schenectady, New York, we retired between ten-thirty and eleven o'clock. The room I slept in was closest to the passage leading to the downstairs, and the two were separated only by a door.

"Once in bed, I found it rather difficult to sleep. As I lay there, I heard a piano playing. It sounded like a very old piano and it played church music. I thought it quite strange that my brother-in-law's father would be listening to his radio at that hour, but felt more annoyed than curious.

"The next morning, as we were having coffee, I mentioned this to my sister. She assured me that her father-in-law would *not* be listening to the radio at that hour and I assured *her* that I *had* heard piano music. It was then she mentioned the old piano her husband's mother had owned for many years and which sat in the downstairs front room.

"We decided to go and have a look at it. The dust that had settled on the keyboard was quite thick, and as definite as they could possibly be were the imprints of someone's fingers. Not normal fingers, but apparently quite thin and bony fingers. My sister's mother-in-law had been terribly thin and she loved to play her piano, especially church music. There was positively no one else in the house who even knew how to play the piano, except my mother, who lived with my sister and her husband."

....

Another New Jersey lady named Louise B., whose full name and address I have in my files, told me of an experience she will never forget.

"I cannot explain why I am sending this on to you, merely that I feel compelled to do so, and after many years of following my compulsions, as I call them, must do so.

"My mother had a bachelor cousin who died and was buried around Valentine's Day, 1932. He had lived with two maiden aunts in Ridgewood, New Jersey, for most of his lifetime. He was a well-known architect in this area. He designed local monuments, one of which is standing in the Park in Ridgewood today. He was short of stature, with piercing eyes and a bushy gray full beard, and he smoked too many cigars. I was not quite 14 years old when he passed away.

"My parents decided to spare me the burial detail, and they left me at home on the way to the cemetery with instructions to stay at home until they returned. They planned on attending the burial, going back to the house with my great-aunts and then coming home before dinner, which in our house was 6 P.M.

"I have no recollection of what I did with my time in the afternoon, but remember that just before dusk I had gone indoors and at the time I was in our dining room, probably setting the table for dinner, as this was one of my chores.

"We had three rooms downstairs: the living room faced north and ran the full length of the house, while the kitchen and dining room faced southeast and southwest respectively, and a T-shaped partition divided the rooms. There was a large archway separating the dining and living rooms.

"I don't recall when I became aware of a 'presence.' I didn't see anything with my eyes, rather I *felt* what I 'saw,' or somehow sensed it and my sense 'saw.' This is not a good explanation, but about the closest I can come to what I felt.

"This presence was not in any one spot in the room, but something that was gradually surrounding me, like the air that I was breathing, and it was frightening and menacing and very evil and stronger, and somehow the word *denser* seemed to apply and I knew that it was 'Uncle' Oscar. I could feel him coming at me from every direction (like music that gets louder and louder), and my senses 'saw' him as he had been dressed in the casket, with a red ribbon draped across his chest, only he was alive and I was aware of some terrible determination on his part and suddenly I knew that somehow he was trying to 'get inside me' and I began to back away. I don't recall speaking, nor his speaking to me. I just knew what his intention was and who he was. I last remember screaming helplessly and uselessly at him to go away. I do not know how long this lasted. I only know that suddenly he was gone, and my parents came into the room. I was hysterical, they tell me, and it took some doing to quiet me."

Many years later Mrs. B. discovered that "Uncle" Oscar had died a raving maniac to the last.

....

Grace Rivers was a secretary by profession, a lady of good background, and not given to hallucinations or emotional outbursts. I had spoken with her several times and always found her most reluctant to discuss what to her seemed incredible.

It seemed that on weekends, Miss Rivers and another secretary, by the name of Juliet, were the house guests of their employer, John Bergner, in Westbrook, Connecticut. Miss Rivers was also a good friend of this furniture manufacturer, a man in his middle fifties. She had joined the Bergner firm in 1948, six years after John Bergner had become the owner of a country house built in 1865.

Bergner liked to spend his weekends among his favorite employees, and sometimes asked some of the office boys as well as his two secretaries to come up to Connecticut with him. All was most idyllic until the early 1950s, when John Bergner met an advertising man by the name of Philip Mervin. This business relationship soon broadened into a social friendship, and before long Mr. Mervin was a steady and often self-invited house guest in Westbrook.

At first, this did not disturb anyone very much, but when Mervin noticed the deep and growing friendship between Bergner and his right-hand girl, something akin to jealousy prompted him to inter-fere with this relationship at every turn. What made this triangle even more difficult for Mervin to bear was the apparent innocence with which Bergner treated Mervin's approaches. Naturally, a feel-ing of dislike grew into hatred between Miss Rivers and the intruder, but before it came to any open argument, the advertising man suddenly died of a heart attack at age 51.

But that did not seem to be the end of it by a long shot.

Soon after his demise, the Connecticut weekends were again interrupted, this time by strange noises no natural cause could account for. Most of the uncanny experiences were witnessed by both girls as well as by some of the office boys, who seemed frightened by it all. With the detachment of a good executive secretary, Miss Rivers lists the phenomena:

Objects moving in space.

Stones hurled at us inside and outside the house.

Clanging of tools in the garage at night (when nobody was there).

Washing machine starting up at 1 A.M., *by itself.*

Heavy footsteps, banging of doors, in the middle of the night.

Television sets turning themselves on and off at will.

A spoon constantly leaping out of a cutlery tray.

The feeling of a cold wind being swept over one.

And there was more, much more.

When a priest was brought to the house to exorcise the ghost, things only got worse. Evidently the deceased had little regard for holy men.

Juliet, the other secretary, brought her husband along. One night in 1962, when Juliet's husband slept in what was once the advertis-ing man's favorite guest room, he heard clearly a series of knocks, as if someone were hitting the top of the bureau. Needless to say, her husband had been alone in the room, and he did not do the knocking.

It became so bad that Grace Rivers no longer looked forward to those weekend invitations at her employer's country home. She feared them. It was then that she remembered, with terrifying suddenness, a remark the late Mr. Mervin had made to her fellow-workers.

"If anything ever happens to me and I die, I'm going to walk after those two girls the rest of their lives!" he had said.

Miss Rivers realized that he was keeping his word.

Her only hope was that the ghost of Mr. Mervin would someday be distracted by an earlier specter that was sharing the house with him. On several occasions, an old woman in black had been seen emerging from a side door of the house. A local man, sitting in front of the house during the weekdays when it was unoccupied — Bergner came up only on weekends — was wondering aloud to Miss Rivers about the "old lady who claimed she occupied the back part of the house." He had encountered her on many occasions, always seeing her disappear into the house by that same, seldom-used, side door. One of the office boys invited by John Bergner also saw her around 1:30 A.M. on a Sunday morning, when he stood outside the house, unable to go to sleep. When she saw him she said hello, and mentioned something about money, then disappeared into a field.

Grace Rivers looked into the background of the house and discovered that it had previously belonged to a very aged man who lived there with his mother. When she died, he found money buried in the house, but he claimed his mother had hidden more money that he had never been able to locate. Evidently the ghost of his mother felt the same way about it, and was still searching. For that's how it is with ghosts sometimes — they become forgetful about material things.

The Ship Chandler's Ghost

*I*t is a well-known fact among ghost hunting experts that structural changes in a house can have dire effects. Take out a wall, and you've got a *poltergeist* mad as a wet hen. I proved that in the case of the Leighton Buzzard ghost in *Ghosts I've Met*. Take down the building, like the studio building at New York's 51 West Tenth Street, and put up a modern apartment house, and you've got no ghost at all. Just a lot of curious tenants. If the ghost is inside the house before the changes are realized, he may bump into walls and doors that weren't there before — not the way he remembered things at all.

But move a whole house several yards away from the shore where it belongs, and you're asking for trouble. Big trouble. And big trouble is what the historical society in Cohasset, Massachusetts, got when they moved the old Ship's Chandlery in Cohasset. With my good friend Bob Kennedy of WBZ, Boston, I set out for the quaint old town south of Boston on a chilly evening in the fall of 1964.

When we arrived at the wooden structure on a corner of the Post Road — it had a nautical look, its two stories squarely set down as if to withstand any gale — we found several people already assembled. Among them were Mrs. E. Stoddard Marsh, the lively curator of the museum, which was what the Ship's Chandlery became, and her associate, lean, quiet Robert Fraser. The others were friends and neighbors who had heard of the coming of a parapsychologist, and didn't want to miss anything. We entered the building and walked around the downstairs portion of it, admiring its displays of nautical supplies, ranging from fishing tackle and scrimshaw made from walrus teeth to heavy anchors, hoists, and rudders — all the instruments and wares of a ship chandler's business.

Built in the late eighteenth century by Samuel Bates, the building was owned by the Bates family; notably by one John Bates, second of the family to have the place, who had died 78 years before our visit. Something of a local character, John Bates had cut a swath around the area as a dashing gentleman. He could well afford the role, for he owned a fishing fleet of 24 vessels, and business was good in those far-off days when the New England coast was dotted with major ports for fishing and shipping. A handwritten record of his daily catch can be seen next to a mysterious closet full of ladies' clothes. Mr. Bates led a full life.

After the arrival of Dorothy Damon, a reporter from the *Boston Traveler*, we started to question the curator about uncanny happenings in the building.

"The building used to be right on the waterfront, at Cohasset Cove, and it had its own pier," Mrs. Marsh began, "and in 1957 we moved it to its present site."

"Was there any report of uncanny happenings before that date?"

"Nothing I know of, but the building was in a bad state of disrepair."

"After the building was brought to its present site, then," I said, "what was the first unusual thing you heard?"

"Two years ago we were having a lecture here. There were about forty people listening to Francis Hagerty talk about old sailing boats. I was sitting over here to the left — on this ground floor — with Robert Fraser, when all of a sudden we heard heavy footsteps upstairs and things being moved and dragged — so I said to Mr. Fraser, 'Someone is up there; will you please tell him to be quiet?' I thought it was kids."

"Did you know whether there was in fact anyone upstairs at the time?"

"We did not know. Mr. Fraser went upstairs and after a moment he came down looking most peculiar and said, 'There is no one there.'"

"Now, there is no other way to get down from upstairs, only this one stairway. Nobody had come down it. We were interrupted three times on that evening."

I asked Robert Fraser what he had seen upstairs.

"There was enough light from the little office that is upstairs, and I could see pretty well upstairs, and I looked all over, but there was nobody upstairs."

"And the other times?"

"Same thing. Windows all closed, too. Nobody could have come down or gotten out. But I'm sure those were footsteps."

I returned to Mrs. Marsh and questioned her further about anything that might have occurred after that eventful evening of footsteps.

"We were kept so busy fixing up the museum that we paid scant attention to anything like that, but this summer something happened that brought it all back to us."

"What happened?" I asked, and the lady reporter perked up her ears.

"It was on one of the few rainy Sundays we had last July," Mrs. Marsh began. "You see, this place is not open on Sundays. I was bringing over some things from the other two buildings, and had my arms full. I opened the front door, when I heard those heavy footsteps upstairs."

"What did you do — drop everything?"

"I thought it was one of our committee or one of the other curators, so I called out, 'Hello — who's up there?' But I got no answer, and I thought, well, someone sure is pretty stuffy, not answering me back, so I was a little peeved and I called again."

"Did you get a reply?"

"No, but *the steps hesitated* when I called. But then they continued again, and I yelled, 'For Heaven's sake, why don't you answer?' — and I went up the stairs, but just as I got to the top of the stairs, they stopped."

There was a man who had helped them with the work at the museum who had lately stayed away for reasons unknown. Could he have heard the footsteps too and decided that caution was the better part of valor?

"The other day, just recently, four of us went into the room this gentleman occupies when he is here, and *the door closed on us*, by itself. It has never done that before."

I soon established that Fraser did not hear the steps when he was *alone* in the building, but that Mrs. Marsh did. I asked her about anything psychic in her background.

"My family has been interested in psychic matters since I was ten years old," she said in a matter-of-fact tone. "I could have become a medium, but I didn't care to. I saw an apparition of my mother immediately after she passed away. My brother also appeared to me six months after his death, to let me know he was all right, I guess."

"Since last July has there been any other manifestation?"

"I haven't been here much," Mrs. Marsh replied. "I had a lot of work with our costume collection in the main building. So I really don't know."

We decided to go upstairs now, and see if Mr. Bates — or whoever the ghost might be — felt like walking for us. We quietly waited in the semi-darkness upstairs, near the area where the footsteps had been heard, but nothing happened.

"The steps went back and forth," Mrs. Marsh reiterated. "Heavy, masculine steps, the kind a big man would make."

She showed us how it sounded, allowing of course for the fact she was wearing high heels. It sounded hollow enough for ten ghosts.

I pointed at a small office in the middle of the upstairs floor.

"This was John Bates' office," Mrs. Marsh explained, "and here is an Indian doll that falls down from a secure shelf now and then as if someone were throwing it."

I examined the doll. It was one of those early nineteenth-century dolls that Indians in New England used to make and sell.

"The people at the lecture also heard the noises," Mrs. Marsh said, "but they just laughed and nobody bothered thinking about it."

I turned to one of the local ladies, a Mrs. Hudley, who had come up with us. Did she feel anything peculiar up here, since she had the reputation of being psychic?

"I feel disturbed. Sort of a strange sensation," she began, haltingly, "as though there was a 'presence' who was in a disturbed frame of mind. It's a man."

Another lady, by the name of McCarthy, also had a strange feeling as we stood around waiting for the ghost to make himself known. Of course, suggestion and atmosphere made me discount most of what those who were around us that night might say, but I still wanted to hear it.

"I felt I had to get to a window and get some air," Mrs. McCarthy said. "The atmosphere seemed disturbed somehow."

I asked them all to be quiet for a moment and addressed myself to the unseen ghost.

"John Bates," I began, "if this is you, may I, as a stranger come to this house in order to help you find peace, ask that you manifest in some form so I know you can hear me?"

Only the sound of a distant car horn answered me.

I repeated my invitation to the ghost to come forward and be counted. Either I addressed myself to the wrong ghost or perhaps John Bates disliked the intrusion of so many people — only silence greeted us.

"Mr. Bates," I said in my most dulcet tones, "please forgive these people for moving your beautiful house inland. They did not do so out of irreverence for your person or work. They did this so that many more people could come and admire your house and come away with a sense of respect and admiration for the great man that you were."

It was so quiet when I spoke, you could have heard a mouse breathe.

Quietly, we tiptoed down the haunted stairs, and out into the cool evening air. Cowboy star Rex Trailer and his wife, who had come with us from Boston, wondered about the future — would the footsteps ever come back? Or was John Bates reconciled with the fact that the sea breezes no longer caressed his ghostly brow as they did when his house was down by the shore?

Then, too, what was the reason he was still around to begin with? Had someone given him his quietus in that little office upstairs? There are rumors of violence in the famous bachelor's life, and the number of women whose affections he had trifled with was legion. Someone might very well have met him one night and ended the highly successful career of the ship chandlery's owner.

A year went by, and I heard nothing further from the curator. Evidently, all was quiet at John Bates' old house. Maybe old John finally joined up with one of the crews that sail the ghost ships on the other side of the curtain of life.

How the Little Girl Ghost Was Sent Out to Play

*E*d Harvey ran a pretty good talk show called "Talk of Philadelphia" on WCAU radio. It was the sort of program people listened to in their homes and cars. They listened in large numbers. I know, for the telephone calls came in fast and furious in the show's final half hour, when calls from the public were answered on the air.

One day in April, 1965, Ed and his charming wife, Marion, went to a cocktail party at a friend's house. There he got to talking to Jack Buffington, who was a regional director of a world-wide relief organization and a pretty down-to-earth fellow, as Ed soon found out. Somehow the talk turned to ghosts, and Buffington had a few things to say on that subject since he lived in a haunted house. At that point, Ed Harvey asked permission for Sybil Leek and myself to come down and have a go at the house.

We arrived at Buffington's house on Lansdowne Avenue, in Lansdowne, a Philadelphia suburb, around 10 o'clock. It was a little hard to find in the dark, and when we got there it did not look ghostly at all, just a nice old Victorian house, big and sprawling. Jack Buffington welcomed us at the door.

As I always do on such occasions, I asked Sybil to wait in another room where she could not hear any of the conversation, while I talked to those who had had experiences in the house.

After Sybil had graciously left, we seated ourselves and took inventory. What I saw was a tastefully furnished Victorian house with several wooden staircases and banisters, and lots of fine small antiques. Our host was joined by his dark-haired Italian-born wife, and two friends from his office. My wife Catherine immediately made friends with Mrs. Buffington, and then we started to find out what this was all about.

The Buffingtons, who had a four-year-old daughter named Allegra, had come to the house just nine months before. A lot had happened to them in those nine months.

"We came home from a trip to Scranton," Jack Buffington began, "and when we got back and I inserted the key in the front door, the hall light went on by itself. It has two switches, one on the upstairs level, so I raced upstairs to see who was in the house, but there was no one there. Periodically this happens, and I thought it was faulty wiring at first, but it has been checked and there is nothing wrong with it. The cellar light and the light in the third floor bathroom also go on and off by themselves. I've seen it, and so have my wife and our little girl."

"Anything else happening here?" I asked casually.

"There are many things that go bump in the night here. The first noise that happened recurrently was the sound of an old treadle sewing machine, which is heard on the average of once every month. This happens in a small room on the second floor, which we now use as a dressing room, but which may well have been a sewing room at one time."

I walked up the narrow stairs and looked at the little room. It had all the marks of a Victorian sewing room where tired servants or a worried mother worked at the clothes for her child.

"It's always around three in the morning, and it awakens us," Mr. Buffington continued, "and then there are footsteps and often they sound like children's footsteps."

"Children's footsteps?"

"Yes, and it is rather startling," Mr. Buffington added, "since we do have a small child in the house and inevitably go and check that it isn't she who is doing it. It never is."

"Is it downstairs?"

"All over the place. There are two stories, or three flights, including the basement. And there are a front and back stairway. There is never any pattern about these things. There may be a lot of happenings at the same time, then there is nothing for weeks, and then it starts again."

"Outside of the child's footsteps, did you ever have any indication of a grown-up presence?" I asked.

"Well, I saw the figure of a woman in the doorway of the dining room, walking down this hall, and through these curtains here, and I heard footsteps in conjunction with it. I thought it was my wife, and I called to her. I was hanging a picture in the dining room at the time. No answer. I was getting annoyed and called her several times over, but there was no response. Finally she answered from the second floor — she had not been downstairs at all."

"What happened to the other woman in the meantime?"

"I walked in here — the hall — and there was no one here."

"How was she dressed?"

"She had on a long skirt, looking like a turn-of-the-century skirt, and she did have her hair on top of her head, and she was tall and slender."

Mrs. Buffington is not very tall, but she does wear dark clothes.

"It was a perfectly solid figure I saw — nothing nebulous or transparent," our host added. "The spring lock at the entrance door was locked securely."

"Did anyone else see an apparition here?"

"My brother met a woman on the stairway — that is, the stairway leading to the third floor. He was spending the night with us, around Thanksgiving time. There was a party that evening and he mistook her for a guest who had somehow remained behind after all the other guests had gone home. She passed him going *up* while he was coming *down*, and she walked into his room, which he thought odd, so he went back to ask if he could help her, but there wasn't anybody there!"

Jack Buffington gave a rather nervous laugh.

I took a good look at the upstairs. Nobody could have gotten out of the house quickly. The stairs were narrow and difficult to negotiate, and the back stairs, in the servants' half of the house, were even more difficult. Anyone descending them rapidly was likely to slip and fall. The two brothers hadn't talked much about all this, I was told, since that time.

"Our little girl must be seeing her, too, for she frequently says she is going up to play with her lady friend," Jack Buffington said.

I started to wander around the house to get the feeling of it. The house was built in 1876 to the specifications of George Penn, a well-known local builder. Although it was now a duplex, it was originally a townhouse for just one family.

The upper stories contained several small, high-ceilinged rooms, and there was about them the forbidding atmosphere of a mid-Victorian house in a small town. The Buffingtons had furnished their house with taste, and the Italian background of the lady of the house was evident in the works of art and antiques strewn about the house.

As I soon discovered, tragedy had befallen the house on Lansdowne Avenue at least twice as far as it was known. The original builder had a sister who suffered from mental illness and was hospitalized many times. She also spent many years in this house. Then a family named Hopkins came to live in it, and it was at that time that the house was divided into two parts. Incidentally, no manifestations had been reported from the other half of the house. About six years before — the exact time was none too clear, and it may be further back — a family named Johnson rented the half now occupied by the Buffingtons. They had a retarded child, a girl, *who was kept locked up in a room on the third floor*. She died in her early teens, they say, in a hospital not far away. Then the house stood empty, looking out onto quiet Lansdowne Avenue with an air of tragedy and secret passion.

Three years went by before the Buffingtons, returning from Italy, took over the house.

"Have there been any unusual manifestations on the third floor?" I asked Mr. Buffington.

"Just one. Something carries on in the trunk up on the third floor. The trunk is empty and there is no reason for those frightful noises. We have both heard it. It is above where the child sleeps."

Mr. Buffington added that a book he read at night in bed often disappeared and showed up in the most peculiar spots around the house — spots that their little four year old couldn't possibly reach. On one occasion, he found it in a bathroom; at least once it traveled from his room upstairs to the top bookshelf downstairs, all by itself.

"My impression of this ghost," Mr. Buffington said, "is that it means no harm. Rather, it has the mischievousness of a child."

I now turned my attention to petite Mrs. Buffington, who had been waiting to tell me of her own most unusual experiences in the house.

"On one occasion I was on the second floor with the child," she began. "It was about eleven in the morning, and I was taking some clothes out of a cabinet. The back staircase is very close to this particular cabinet. Suddenly, I very distinctly heard a voice calling 'Mamma,' a voice of a person standing close to the cabinet, and it was a girl's voice, a child's voice and quite distinct — in fact, my daughter, Allegra, also heard it, for she turned to me and asked 'Mammi, who is it?'"

"What did you do?"

"I pretended to be nonchalant about it, looked all over, went up the stairs, opened cabinets — but, of course, there was no one there."

"And your daughter?"

"When we did not find anyone, she said, 'Oh, it must be our lady upstairs.'"

"Any other experiences you can recall?"

"Yes, tonight, in fact," Mrs. Buffington replied. "I was in the kitchen feeding the child, and I was putting something into the garbage container, when I heard a child's voice saying 'It's lower down' — just that, nothing more."

"Amazing," I conceded.

"It was a young girl's voice," Mrs. Buffington added. "I looked at Allegra, but it was obvious to me that the voice had come from the opposite direction. At any rate, Allegra was busy eating. I've been very nervous the past few days and about a week ago, when my husband was away in Washington, I spent the night alone, and having had some strong coffee, could not find sleep right away. I had moved the child in with me, so I did not have to stay by myself. I switched the light off, and the door to the landing of the second floor staircase was open. Just on that spot I suddenly heard those crashing noises as if somebody were rolling down. I was terrified. As soon as I switched the light back on, it stopped. There was nothing on the stairs. I sat on the bed for a moment, then decided it was my nerves, and turned the light off again. Immediately, the same noise returned, even louder. There was no mistaking the origin of the noises this time. They came from the stairs in front of the room. I switched the light on again and they stopped, and I left the lights burning the rest of the night. I finally fell asleep from sheer exhaustion."

"One more thing," Jack Buffington broke in. "On the back staircase, there is an area about four feet long which is a terribly frigid area sporadically. My little girl wouldn't walk up that staircase if she could possibly help it. Both my wife and I felt the cold spot."

"Is this in the area of the room where the little child was kept?" I asked.

"It is one floor below it, but it is the area, yes," Mrs. Buffington admitted.

I had heard enough by now to call in Sybil Leek, who had been outside waiting patiently for the call to lend her considerable psychic talents to the case.

After she had seated herself in one of the comfortable leather chairs, and we had grouped ourselves around her in the usual fashion, I quickly placed her into trance. Within a few minutes, her lips started to quiver gently, and then a voice broke through.

"Can't play," a plaintive child's voice said.

"Why not?" I asked immediately, bringing the microphone close to Sybil's entranced lips to catch every word.

"No one to play with. I want to play."

"Who do you want to play with?"

"Anyone. I don't like being alone."

"What is your name?"

"Elizabeth."

"What is your family name?"

"Streiber."

"How old are you?"

"Nine."

"What is your father's name?"

"Joseph Streiber."

Now Sybil had no knowledge that a child's ghost had been heard in the house. Nor had she overheard our conversation about it. Yet, the very first to manifest when trance had set in was a little girl!

I continued to question her.

"Your mother's name?"

"Mammi."

"What is her first name?"

The child thought for a moment, as if searching, then repeated:

"Mammi."

With sudden impact, I thought of the ghostly voice calling for "Mamma" heard on the steps by Mrs. Buffington and her little daughter.

"Do you go to school?"

The answer was almost angry.

"No! I play."

"Where do you live in this house?"

"Funny house . . . I get lost . . . too big."

"Where is your room?"

"On the stairs."

"Who else lives in the house?"

"Mammi."

"Anyone else?"

"No one."

"Where were you born?"

"Here."

"What is your birthday?"

"Eight . . . Eighteen . . . Twenty-One."

"What month?"

"March."

Did she mean that she was born in 1821? The house was built in 1876 and before that time, only a field existed on the site. Or was she trying to say: March 8th, 1921? Dates always confuse a ghost, I have found.

"Are you feeling well?"

A plaintive "no" was the answer. What was wrong with her, I wanted to know.

"I slip on the stairs," the ghost said. "I slipped down the stairs. I like to do that."

"Did you get hurt?"

"Yes."

"What happened then?"

"So I sit on the stairs," the little girl ghost said, "and sometimes I run down one staircase. Not the other. Then I have fun."

"Is there anyone else with you?"

"Mammi."

Again I thought of the apparition in the Victorian dress Jack Buffington had seen in the hall.

"Do you see her now?" I asked.

An emphatic "no" was the answer.

"When have you seen her last?"

She thought that one over for a moment.

"Two days."

"Is she living?"

"Yes . . . she goes away, and then I'm lost."

"Does she come back?"

"Yes."

"What about your father?"

"Don't like my father. Not very nice time with my father. He shouts."

"What floor is your room on?"

"At the top."

I recalled that the retarded little girl had been kept in a locked room on the top floor.

"Do you ever go downstairs?"

"Of course I go downstairs. I play on the stairs. And I'm going to sit on the stairs all the time until somebody plays with me!"

"Isn't there any other little girl or boy around?" I asked.

"I don't get at him . . . they take him away and hide him."

"Who does?"

"People here."

"Do you see people?"

"Yes."

"Do people see *you?*"

"They think they do . . . they're not very nice, really."

"Do you talk to them?" She seemed to nod. "What do you tell them?"

"I want to play."

"Do you call out for anyone?" I asked.

"Mammi."

"Is there anyone else in this house you can see? Any children?"

"Yes, but they won't play."

"What sort of children are there in this house?"

"They won't play."

How do you explain to a child that she is a ghost?

"Would you like to meet some other children like yourself who do want to play?" I asked. She liked that very much. I told her to imagine such children at play and to think of nothing else. But she wanted to play in this house.

"I live here."

I persisted in telling her that there were children outside, in a beautiful meadow, just waiting for her to join them.

"My father tells me not to."

"But he is not here."

"Sometimes I see him."

"Come outside now."

"I don't go outside in the daytime."

"What do you do in the daytime then?"

"I get up early and play on the stairs."

She was afraid to go outside, she said, but preferred to wait for "them" in the house, so she would not miss them. I explained things to her ever so gently. She listened. Eventually, she was willing to go, wondering only — "When do I come back?"

"You won't want to come back, Elizabeth," I replied, and asked if she understood these things now.

She thought for a moment, then said:

"Funny man . . . "

"You see, something happened to you, and you are not quite the same as before," I tried to explain. "People in this house are not like you and that's why you can't play with them. But outside in the meadow there are many like you. Children to play with all your life!"

And then I sent her away.

There was a strange, rapping noise on the staircase now, as if someone were saying good-bye in a hurry. Abruptly, the noise ceased and I recalled Sybil, still entranced, to her own body.

I asked her to describe what she saw on her side of the veil.

"The child is difficult," she said. "Doesn't want to leave the house. She's frightened of her father. She's about ten. Died here, fell."

I instructed the medium to help the child out of the house and across the border. This she did.

"There is also a woman here," Sybil said. "I think she followed the child. She is tied to this house because the child would not go."

"What does she look like?"

"Medium fair, full face, not thin — she wears a green dress in one piece, dark dress — she comes and goes — she worries about the child — I think *she left the child*."

Guilt, I thought, so often the cause of a haunting!

"When she came back, something had happened," Sybil continued. "The child had been injured and now she keeps coming back to find the child. But the child only wants to play and sit on the stairs."

"Can you contact the woman for us?" I asked.

"The woman is not a good person," Sybil replied slowly. "She is sorry. She listens now."

"Tell her we've sent the child away."

"She knows."

"Tell her she need no longer haunt this house; her guilt feelings are a matter of the past."

"She wants to follow the child. She wants to go now."

"She should think of the child with love, and she will join her."

"She doesn't love the child."

"She will have to desire to see her family again, then, to cross over. Instruct her."

In a quiet voice, Sybil suggested to the ghost that she must go from the house and never return here.

"She won't upset the house, now that the child is gone," Sybil assured us. "The search for the child was the cause of it all."

"Was the child ill?" I asked.

"The child was difficult and lonely, and she fell."

Again I heard rapping noises for a moment.

"Was there anything wrong with this child?"

"I'm not so sure. I think she was a little *fou*. She was florid, you know, nobody to look after her, looking for things all the time and frightened to go out."

"Did she die in this house or was she taken somewhere?"

"She died here."

Sometimes the ghost reattaches himself to the last refuge he had on the earth plane, even though the body may expire elsewhere, and instantly returns to that place, never to leave it again, until freed by someone like myself.

"The woman is gone now," Sybil mumbled. "The child went a long way, and the woman is gone now, too."

I thanked Sybil and led her back to consciousness, step by step, until she woke up in the present, fully relaxed as if after a good night's rest, and, of course, not remembering a thing that had come through her entranced lips the past hour.

Mr. Buffington got up, since the spell of the foregoing had been broken, and motioned me to follow him to the next room.

"There is something I just remembered," he said. "My daughter, Allegra, took a fall on the staircase on the spot where those chills have been felt. She wore one of her mother's high heels and the likelihood of a spill was plausible — still, it was on *that* very spot."

The next morning, I called a number of people who knew Lansdowne history and past residents well enough to be called experts. I spoke to the librarian at the Chester County Historical Society and the librarian at Media, and to a long-time resident Mrs. Susan Worell, but none of them knew of a Joseph Streiber with a little girl named Elizabeth. The records back into the twenties or even earlier are pretty scanty in this area and research was almost hopeless. Quite conceivably, the Streibers were among the tenants who had the house in a transitory way during the years of which Jack Buffington had no records — but then again, there are certain parallels between fact and trance results that cannot be dismissed lightly.

Jack Buffington thought the description of the woman he saw and that given by the medium do not fully correspond, but then he did not see the specter long enough to be really sure.

The retarded child Sybil Leek brought through had an amazing similarity to the actual retarded girl of about ten who had lived in the house and died in a nearby hospital, and the word "Mamma" that Mrs. Buffington had heard so clearly was also close to what the ghost girl said she kept calling her mother.

There was some mystery about the dates — and even the long-time residents of the area I interviewed could not help me pin down the facts. Was there a man by that name with a little girl?

Records were not well kept in this respect and people in America could come and go far more easily than in European countries, for instance, where there was an official duty to report one's moves to either the police or some other government office.

A day or two after our visit, Jack Buffington reported that the noises were worse than ever! It was as if our contact with the wraiths had unleashed their fury; having been told the truth about their status, they would naturally have a feeling of frustration and resentment, or at least the woman would. This resentment often occurs after an investigation in which trance contact is made. But eventually things quiet down and I had the feeling that the woman's guilt feelings would also cease. That the little girl ghost had been sent out to play, I have no doubt. Perhaps that aftermath was the mother's fury at having her no longer in her sight. But then I never said that ghosts are the easiest people to live with.

The Ghost-Servant Problem at Ringwood Manor

Ringwood, in the south of England, has an American counterpart in New Jersey. I had never heard of Ringwood Manor in New Jersey until Mrs. Edward Tholl, a resident of nearby Saddle River, brought it to my attention. An avid history buff and a talented geographer and map maker, Mrs. Tholl had been to the Manor House and on several occasions felt "a presence." The mountain people who still inhabited the Ramapo Mountains of the region wouldn't go near the Manor House at night.

"Robert Erskine, geographer to Washington's army, is buried on the grounds," Mrs. Tholl told me.

The Manor House land was purchased by the Ogden family of Newark in 1740, and an iron-smelting furnace was built on it two years later. The area abounds in mine deposits and was at one time a center of iron mining and smelting. In 1762, when a second furnace was built, a small house was also built. This house still stands and now forms part of the haphazard arrangement that constitutes the Manor House today. One Peter Hasenclever bought the house and iron works in 1764. He ran the enterprise with such ostentation that he was known as "The Baron." But Hasenclever did not produce enough iron to suit his backers, and was soon replaced by Robert Erskine. When the War of Independence broke out, the iron works were forced to close. Erskine himself died "of exposure" in 1780.

By 1807, the iron business was going full blast again, this time under the aegis of Martin Ryerson, who tore down the ramshackle old house and rebuilt it completely. After the iron business failed in the 1830s, the property passed into the hands of famed Peter Cooper in 1853. His son-in-law Abram S. Hewitt, one-time Mayor of New York, lived in the Manor House.

Mrs. Hewitt, Cooper's daughter, turned the drab house into an impressive mansion of 51 rooms, very much as it appears today. Various older buildings already on the grounds were uprooted and added to the house, giving it a checkered character without a real center. The Hewitt family continued to live at Ringwood until Erskine Hewitt deeded the estate to the State of New Jersey in 1936, and the mansion became a museum through which visitors were shown daily for a small fee.

During troubled times, tragedies may well have occurred in and around the house. There was a holdup in 1778, and in the graveyard nearby, many French soldiers were buried who died there during an epidemic. There is also on record an incident, in later years, when a cook was threatened by a butler with a knife, and there were disasters that took many lives in the nearby iron mines.

One of the Hewitt girls, Sally, had been particularly given to mischief. If anyone were to haunt the place, she'd be a prime candidate for the job. I thanked Claire Tholl for her help, and called on Ethel Johnson Meyers to accompany me to New Jersey. Of course, I didn't give her any details. We arranged to get to the house around dusk, after all the tourists had gone.

My wife Catherine and I, with Ethel Meyers as passenger, drove out to the house on a humid afternoon in May, 1965. Jim Byrne joined us at the house with *Saturday Review* writer Haskell Frankel in tow.

We were about an hour late, but it was still light, and the peaceful setting of the park with the Manor House in its center reminded one indeed of similar houses gracing the English countryside.

We stood around battling New Jersey mosquitoes for a while, then I asked Catherine to take Ethel away from the house for a moment, so I could talk to Mrs. Tholl and others who had witnessed ghostly goings-on in the house.

"I've had a feeling in certain parts of the house that I was not alone," Mrs. Tholl said, "but other than that I cannot honestly say I have had uncanny experiences here."

Alexander Waldron had been the superintendent of Ringwood Manor for many years, until a year before, in fact. He consented to join us for the occasion. A jovial, gray-haired man, he seemed rather deliberate in his report, giving me only what to him were actual facts.

"I was superintendent here for eighteen years," Mr. Waldron began. "I was sitting at my desk one day, in the late afternoon, like today, and the door to the next room was closed. My office is on the ground floor. I heard two people come walking toward me at a fast pace. That did not seem unusual, for we do have workmen here frequently. When the steps reached my door, nothing happened. Without thinking too much, I opened the door for them. But there was no one there. I called out, but there was no answer. Shortly after, two workmen did come in from outside, and together we searched the whole building, but found no one who could have made the sound."

"Could anyone have walked away without being seen by you?"

"Impossible. There was good light."

"Did anything else happen after that?"

"Over the years we've had a few things we could not explain. For instance, doors we had shut at night, we found open the next morning. Some years ago, when I had my boys living here with me, they decided to build a so-called monster down in the basement. One boy was of high-school age, the other in grammar school — sixteen and thirteen. One of them came in by himself one night, when he heard footsteps overhead, on the ground floor. He thought it was his brother who had come over from the house.

"He thought his brother was just trying to scare him, so he continued to work downstairs. But the footsteps continued and finally he got fed up with it and came upstairs. All was dark, and nobody was around. He ran back to the house, where he found his brother, who had never been to the Manor at all."

Bradley Waldron probably never worked on his "monster" again after that.

There are stories among the local hill folk of Robert Erskine's ghost walking with a lantern, or sitting on his grave half a mile down the road from the Manor House, or racing up the staircase in the house itself.

Wayne Daniels, who had accompanied Mrs. Tholl to the House, spoke up now. Mr. Daniels had lived in the region all his life, and was a professional restorer of early American structures.

"I have felt strange in one corner of the old dining room, and in two rooms upstairs," he volunteered. "I feel hostility in those areas, somehow."

It was time to begin our search in the house itself.

I asked Ethel Meyers to join us, and we entered the Manor House, making our way slowly along the now-deserted corridors and passages of the ground floor, following Ethel as she began to get her psychic bearings.

Suddenly, Ethel remarked that she felt a man outside the windows, but could not pin down her impression.

"Someone died under a curse around here," she mumbled, then

added as if it were an afterthought, "Jackson White . . . what does that mean?"

I had never heard the name before, but Claire Tholl explained that "Jackson White" was a peculiar local name for people of mixed blood, who live in the Ramapo hills. Ethel added that someone had been in slavery at one time.

Ethel was taken aback by the explanation of "Jackson White." She had taken it for granted that it was an individual name. Jackson Whites, I gathered, are partly American Indian and partly black, but not white.

We now entered a large bedroom elegantly furnished in the manner of the early nineteenth century, with a large bed against one wall and a table against the other. Ethel looked around the room uncertainly, as if looking for something she did not yet see.

"Someone with a bad conscience died in this room," she said. "A man and a woman lived here, who were miles apart somehow."

It was Mrs. Erskine's bedroom we were in. We went through a small door into another room that lay directly behind the rather large bedroom; it must have been a servant's room at one time. Nevertheless, it was elegant, with a marble fireplace and a heavy oak table, around which a number of chairs had been placed. We sat down but before I had time to adjust my tape recorder and camera, Ethel Meyers fell into deep trance. From her lips came the well-modulated voice of Albert, her control. He explained that several layers of consciousness covered the room, that there were blacks brought here by one Jackson, who came in the eighteenth century. One of them seemed present in the room, he felt.

"One met death at the entrance . . . a woman named Lucy Bell, she says. She was a servant here."

Suddenly, Albert was gone. In his stead, there was a shrill, desperate female voice, crying out to all who would listen.

"No . . . I didn't . . . before my God I didn't . . . I show you where . . . I didn't touch it . . . never . . ."

She seemed to be speaking to an unseen tormentor now, for Ethel, possessed by the ghost, pulled back from the table and cried:

"No . . . don't . . . don't!" Was she being beaten or tortured?

"He didn't either!" the ghost added.

I tried to calm her.

"I didn't touch . . . I didn't touch . . ." she kept repeating.

I asked for her name.

"Lucy," she said in a tormented, high-pitched voice completely different from Ethel Meyers' normal tones.

"I believe you," I said, and told the ghost who we were and why we had come. The uncontrollable crying subsided for the moment.

"He's innocent too," she finally said. "I can't walk," she added. Ethel pointed to her side. Had she been hurt?

"I didn't take it," she reiterated. "It's right there."

What didn't she take? I coaxed her gently to tell me all about it.

"I've come as a *friend*," I said, and the word finally hit home. She got very excited and wanted to know where I was since she could not see me.

"A friend, Jeremiah, do you hear?" she intoned.

"Who is Jeremiah?"

"He didn't do it either," she replied. Jeremiah, I gathered, lived here, too, but she did not know any family name — just Jeremiah. Then Ethel Meyers grabbed my hand, mumbling "friend," and almost crushed my fingers. I managed to pull it away. Ethel ordinarily has a very feminine, soft grip — a great contrast to the desperately fierce clasp of the ghost possessing the medium!

"Don't go!"

I promised to stay if she would talk.

"I have never stolen," she said. "It's dark . . . I can't see now . . . where do I go to see always?"

"I will show you the way," I promised.

"Marie . . . Marie . . . where are you?" she intoned pleadingly.

"What is Jeremiah doing?"

"He is begging for his honor."

"Where is he now?"

"Here with me."

"Who is the person you worked for?" I asked.

"Old lady . . . I don't want her . . . "

"If she did you wrong, should we punish her? What is her name?"

"I never wished evil on anyone . . . I would forgive her . . . if she forgives me. She is here . . . I saw her, and she hates me . . . "

The voice became shrill and emotional again. I started to send her away, and in a few moments, she slipped out. Suddenly, there was an entirely different person occupying Ethel's body. Proudly sitting up, she seemed to eye us, with closed eyes, of course, as if we were riff-raff invading her precincts.

"What is your name?" I demanded.

"I am in no court of justice," was the stiff reply in a proper upper-middle-class accent. "I cannot speak to you. I have no desire. It is futile for you to give me any advice."

"What about this servant girl?" I asked.

"You may take yourself away," the lady replied, haughtily. "Depart!"

"What did the girl take?" I asked, ignoring her outburst of cold fury.

"I am not divulging anything to you."

"Is she innocent then?"

This gave her some thought, and the next words were a little more communicative.

"How come you are in my house?" she demanded.

"Is it your house?"

"I will call the servants and have you taken out by the scruff of your neck," she threatened.

"Will the servants know who you are?" I countered.

"I am lady in my own."

"What is your name?"

"I refuse to reveal myself or talk to you!"

I explained about the passage of time. It made no impression.

"I will call her . . . Old Jeremiah is under his own disgrace. You are friend to him?"

I explained about Ethel Meyers and how she, the ghost, was able to communicate with us.

She hit the table hard with Ethel's fist.

"The man is mad," the ghost said. "Take him away!"

I didn't intend to be taken away by ghostly men-in-white. I continued to plead with "the lady" to come to her senses and listen. She kept calling for her servants, but evidently nobody answered her calls.

"Jeremiah, if you want to preserve yourself in my estimation and not stand by this girl, take this . . . "

Somehow the medium's eyes opened for a moment, and the ghost could "see." Then they closed again. It came as a shock, for "the lady" suddenly stopped her angry denunciation and instead "looked" at me in panic.

"What is this? Doctor . . . where is he . . . Laura! Laura! I am ill. Very ill. I can't see. I can't see. I hear something talking to me, but I can't see it. Laura, call a doctor. I'm going to die!"

"As a matter of fact," I said calmly, "you have died already."

"It was my mother's." The ghost sobbed hysterically. "Don't let her keep it. Don't let it go to the scum! I must have it. Don't let me die like this. Oh, oh . . . "

I called on Albert, the control, to take the unhappy ghost away and lead her to the other side of the veil, if possible. The sobbing slowly subsided as the ghost's essence drifted away out of our reach in that chilly Georgian room at Ringwood.

It wasn't Albert's crisp, precise voice that answered me. Another stranger, obviously male, now made his coughing entry and spoke in a lower-class accent.

"What's the matter?"

"Who is this?" I asked.

The voice sounded strangely muffled, as if coming from far away.

"Jeremiah . . . What's the matter with everybody?" The voice had distinct black overtones.

"I'm so sleepy," the voice said.

"Who owns this house?"

"Ho, ho, I do," the ghost said. "I have a funny dream, what's the matter with everybody?" Then the voice cleared up a little, as he became more aware of the strange surroundings into which he had entered.

"Are you one of these white trashes?" he demanded.

"What is the old lady's name?" I asked.

"She's a Bob," he replied, enigmatically, and added, "real bumby, with many knots in it, many knots in the brain."

"Who else is here?"

"I don't like you. I don't know you and I don't like who I don't know," the servant's ghost said.

"You're white trash," he continued. "I seed you!" The stress was on *white*.

"How long have you been living here?"

"My father . . . Luke."

Again, I explained about death and consequences, but the reception was even less friendly than I had received from "the lady."

Jeremiah wanted no truck with death.

"What will the old squaw say? What will she say?" he wondered. "She needs me."

"Not really," I replied. "After all, she's dead, too." He could hardly believe the news. Evidently, the formidable "squaw" was immune to such events as death in his mind.

"What do you have against my mother?" he demanded now. Things were getting confusing. Was the "old lady" his mother?

"Lucy white trash too," he commented.

"Was she your wife?"

"Call it that."

"Can you see her?"

"She's here."

"Then you know you have died and must go from this house?" I asked.

"'dominable treek, man, 'dominable treek," he said, furiously.

"This house is no longer yours."

"It never was," he shot back. "The squaw is here. We're not dead, great white spirit — laugh at you."

"What do you want in this house?"

"Squaw very good," he said. "I tell you, my mother, squaw very good. Lucy Bell, white trash, but good. Like Great White Spirit. Work my fingers down to the bone. I am told! I am thief, too. Just yesterday. Look at my back! Look at my squaw! Red Fox, look at her. Look at my back, look at it!"

He seemed to have spent his anger. The voice became softer now.

"I am so sleepy," he said. "So sleepy . . . my Lucy will never walk again . . . angel spirit . . . my people suffer . . . her skin should be like mine . . . help me, help my Lucy. . . ."

I promised to help and to send him to his father, Luke, who was awaiting him.

"I should have listened to my father," the ghost mumbled.

Then he recognized his father, evidently come to guide him out of the house, and wondered what he was doing here.

I explained what I thought was the reason for his father's presence. There was some crying, and then they all went away.

"Albert," I said. "Please take over the instrument."

In a moment, the control's cool voice was heard, and Ethel was brought out of trance rather quickly.

"My hip," she complained. "I don't think I can move."

"Passing conditions" or symptoms the ghost brings are sometimes present for a few moments after a medium comes out of trance. It is nothing to be alarmed about.

I closed Ethel's eyes again, and sent her back into trance, then brought her out again, and this time all was "clear." However, she still recalled a scream in a passage between the two rooms.

I wondered about the Indian nature of the ghost. Were there any Indians in this area?

"Certainly," Mr. Waldron replied. "They are of mixed blood, often Negro blood, and are called Jackson Whites. Many of them worked here as servants."

The footsteps the superintendent had heard on the floor below were of two persons, and they could very well have come from this area, since the room we were in was almost directly above his offices.

There was, of course, no record of any servants named Jeremiah or Lucy. Servants' names rarely get recorded unless they do something that is most unusual.

I asked Mrs. Tholl about ladies who might have fitted the description of the haughty lady who had spoken to us through Ethel Meyers in trance.

"I associate this with the Hewitt occupancy of the house," she explained, "because of the reference to a passage connecting two parts of the house, something that could not apply to an early structure on the spot. Amelia Hewitt, whose bedroom we had come through, was described in literature of the period as 'all placidity and kindliness.' Sarah Hewitt, however, was quite a cut-up in her day, and fitted the character of 'the lady' more accurately."

But we cannot be sure of the identity of the ghost-lady. She elected to keep her name a secret and we can only bow to her decision and let it remain so.

What lends the accounts an air of reality and evidence is, of course, the amazing fact that Ethel Meyers spoke of "Jackson Whites" in this house, an appellation completely new to her and me.

I am also sure that the medium had no knowledge of Indians living in the area. Then, too, her selecting a room above the spot where the ghostly steps had been heard was interesting, for the house was sprawling and had many rooms and passages.

Return to Clinton Court

When I investigated Clinton Court, New York, in 1960, and wrote about it in *Ghost Hunter*, I never dreamed I'd have to come back and talk to a ghost again. But sometimes the dead won't stay still. Our first visit had been somewhat impaired by a nervous real estate firm who wanted us out of the house as quickly as possible. Ethel Johnson Meyers went into trance in the lower portion of what was once the stables and carriage house of Governor Clinton. Now located in the heart of Hell's Kitchen, it was then a rural neighborhood in which the Clinton Mansion, now gone, was surrounded by fields and woodlands close to the North River.

Ethel Meyers' trance was fully described in the chapter called "The Clinton Court Ghosts" in *Ghost Hunter*. When we left the downstairs apartment where Ethel and I had spent a quiet hour, I was pretty sure there would be no further need for our services. The apartment was then in a state of disrepair, there was no tenant as yet, and all we had to sit on were a bench and a completely worn-out chair someone had left behind.

I thought no more of charming Clinton Court so neatly tucked away behind an iron gate and probably unknown to most New

Yorkers, until 1964, when a Miss Alyce Montreuil wrote to me of her experiences in the house at 422½ West Forty-sixth Street, New York.

As a friend of the tenants who had taken one of the two apartments making up the former carriage house, she had had her brush with the uncanny. I reported this in detail in *Ghosts I've Met*; how the upstairs door near the porch atop the stairs would not stay closed, how the door seemingly unlocked itself, and how her dogs would freeze when approaching the staircase leading to the upper apartment.

Again I thought I had done my duty to restless Clinton Court by reporting these later developments during the tenancy of Danny Brown and Frank Benner, between 1959 and 1963. Meanwhile, the lower apartment had also acquired new tenants, Mr. and Mrs. Dan Neary, who had lived there since 1963.

Somehow Clinton Court would not leave me alone. A young student of the occult named Bob Nelson wrote to me of doors opening by themselves. But he had read my book, and I was afraid it might have inspired him to look for these things. Then in February of 1965, Mrs. Leo Herbert contacted me after seeing Sybil Leek and myself "de-ghosting" (or trying to "de-ghost") June Havoc's house, situated behind theirs, on Miss Havoc's television program.

Her husband, a direct descendant of Victor Herbert, was property master for all David Merrick shows, and Mrs. Herbert was a dancer. They had lived in the two top floors composing the upper apartment since 1964. There were some odd things going on in the place, and would Sybil Leek and I please come and have a talk with whoever it was who was causing them?

No sooner said than done. On March 28, about a dozen people assembled in the upstairs living room of the Herberts. They included the downstairs neighbors, the Nearys; some people living in the front, or un-haunted section of Clinton Court; Bob Nelson, Carl Gewritz, the Herbert children, and Mr. and Mrs. Biff Liff; Gail Benedict, public relations director, Bill Hazlett, and Peter Hahn of

North American Newspaper Alliance; Catherine and I; and, of course, Sybil Leek, resplendent in purple dress, stockings, and cape.

Promptly at nine, we dimmed the lights and grouped ourselves around the room roughly in a circle, with Sybil stretching out on a chair in the upper center.

After the usual few moments of hypnosis, I had Sybil safely entranced, and I waited for the ghost to make himself or herself known. I knew there were several layers of consciousness in the place, and I could not be sure about the ones who would break through the barrier and use Sybil's vocal cords to communicate with us.

Her lips moved silently for a few moments while I strained not to miss the first words. Gradually the sounds became intelligible and I moved closer.

"What is your name?" I asked.

"Walker."

I asked the ghost to speak up.

"George . . . Walker," the voice said, plainly now.

"Is this your house?"

"No. George . . . I have blood in my mouth . . . hurt."

"Who hurt you?"

"Don't know . . . dying . . . I'm dying . . . too late . . . "

"Do you live here?"

"No . . . Brice."

"What street?"

"No street. Brice. South."

"What year is this?"

"Ninety-two."

"What can we do to help you?"

"I want to live . . . doctor."

"Which doctor do you want us to call?"

"Warren. East . . . Easton."

It sounded like East Hampton to me, but I wasn't sure. The voice had difficulty maintaining an even tone.

"How did you get to this house?" I inquired.

"Went to the river . . . everybody . . . friends, soldiers . . . Alfred . . . came to rest . . ."

"Why did you come to this house?"

"I like it . . . remembered . . . coming here to see George . . . two Georgies."

"What is this other George's name?"

"Clinton. George Clinton . . . I die . . . "

"Are you a soldier?"

"Yeah . . . Colonel . . . George . . . Walker."

"What regiment?"

"Two-Four."

"Who is the commanding general?"

"Wilson."

"First name?"

"Amos . . . nobody bothers . . ."

"Yes, I do. I will help you. Who attacked you?"

"I don't know."

I asked what he wanted in this house.

"I want to stay . . . no house, field! Can't get to the house."

"Where were you born?" I changed the subject before the ghost could get too upset to give us information.

"Brice . . . Carolina . . . "

"When did you come up here?"

The voice hesitated.

"Eight-three . . . no, ninety-three . . . eighty-eight."

"How did you get hurt?"

"Blood in my chest . . . knife . . ." He added that it was a man, a soldier, but he did not recognize him.

Suddenly, the jaws of the medium started to quiver and the voice began to give out.

"Can't talk . . ." I calmed him, and his tone became once more steadier.

"What other regiments were here?" I resumed.

"Queens . . . Nine . . ."

"Were you in any campaign?"

"Brice . . ."

"What town is Brice near?"

"Pike's Hill."

"What colony?"

"Carolina . . . North Carolina."

"Any other town it is near to?"

"Pike's Hill, Three Hills . . ."

I asked him whether he knew anyone else here, but the ghost replied he couldn't see things in the "field," only smoke.

"The house is too far. I can't get there," he repeated.

"What is your wife's name?"

"Martha . . . Brice."

"Children?"

"Three."

"Your father's name?"

"Stephen . . . Brice . . . Burnt Oak . . . ."

"Is that the name of a house?"

"Yes . . ."

"Is he alive or dead?"

"Dead."

"When did he die?"

"Fifty-nine."

"Where is he buried?"

"Burnt Oak."

"Cemetery?"

"In the garden."

"What denomination was he?"

"Catholic."

"Were you Catholic?"

"Yes . . . French Catholic."

"Were you baptized?"

"St. Theresa."

"Where is this?"

"Pike Hill."

"What year were you born?"

"Thirty-four."

"Any brothers who were officers?"

"Clifford . . . Colonel . . . fourteenth regiment, stationed Pike Hill."

"Cavalry or infantry?"

"Infantry."

"Any other brothers who were officers?"

"Aaron . . . Captain . . . "

"Where stationed?"

"Don't know."

I felt it was time to release this unhappy one. Gently, I suggested his pain was no more, and asked him to join his loved ones.

A moment later he slipped away. I then asked that Sybil Leek, still deeply entranced, answer my questions, without awakening. This is actually switching from deep trance to clairvoyant trance in the middle of the séance, but Sybil has extraordinary powers of the mind and is a disciplined medium. Sybil's own voice responded to me now. She sounded somewhat sleepy and wasn't her usual crisp self, but nevertheless she was clearly audible.

I asked her to look around and report what she saw. Sybil's etheric body was now "on the other side" for the time being, and she was able to see the same things a permanent resident of that other world would be seeing.

She described a house with three windows, with a "sort of office" inside.

"There are people here who should not be here . . . girls!" she said.

"What happens here?" I asked.

"Something to do with the staircase . . . something happened . . . trying to see . . . I don't like it . . . someone hanging . . . don't like it . . . a man . . . ''

"What does he look like?"

"Six . . . young men . . . gray clothes . . . someone hung *him* . . . I don't want to look . . . ."

"Is there anyone else on the staircase?" I inquired.

"Yes," Sybil said in halting tones. "That girl."

"How old is she?"

"Twenty-five, twenty-six."

"What is she doing on the staircase?"

"She has seen *him*. Doesn't care. She wants someone to take him away, but then she forgets about it. She was wrong about the man . . . liking him . . . I see her living in this house and she is very happy, until she gets frightened by the man. She doesn't like the staircase. Someone takes the staircase and *puts it somewhere else* . . . I don't want to stay here . . . bad house."

"What about the staircase?" I pressed Sybil.

"She moved the staircase and then got to go back to the old staircase and then they caught up with her."

"Who caught up with her?"

"The man's friends. The man who was hung. She was very ill. He had her move the staircase. They knew it was there. And so she kept going back. And then she died . . . *somebody pushed her*. And she hurt her back, she couldn't walk, bad house."

"The girl — because she's frightened. She throws things onto the ground. She runs up the stairs — the other stairs — trying to get away — she doesn't like music — reminds her of sad song — the music starts things off here."

"How long ago did she die?"

"Eighteen-four-o — about . . . ''

"Is she causing all the disturbances in this house?" I asked.

"No . . . a man, and she, and others . . . lot of people pass through . . . to the river."

"Anyone else on the staircase?"

"No."

"Look at the door. Is anybody at the door?"

"Animal . . . dog . . . scratching . . . nobody there to let it in . . . she's inside."

"Is this her house?"

"Sort of. Lives here . . . .Goes to the door because of the scratching noise."

"Is it her dog?"

"Dog lives in the house . . . strange, she wants to go, and she can't."

"Why?"

"Because she would have no money. She is wanting to open the door, let the dog in."

"Is the woman on the other side?"

Sybil's voice was somewhat puzzled.

"*I'm* on the other side."

Of course she was . . . temporarily.

"Is she the same girl you saw on the stairs?"

"Yes."

"Is there anyone else here?"

"No."

"Do you see any children here?"

"Four children. Not here now. Not very strong."

"Look at the staircase once more. Was there any kind of tragedy on this staircase?"

"I see someone who falls. Older man. The girl . . . is used to the staircase now. She keeps *staying* on this staircase."

"You mean like the man who was hanged?"

"Yes. It is very confusing. She is on the staircase waiting for something else, I think. Someone and something else to happen. Someone to come, she is very confused."

I felt Sybil had been "under" long enough and decided to bring her out of her trance. This was accomplished quickly. When Sybil awoke, she remembered very little, as usual.

The group was animated now as everyone sought to sum up reactions and feelings. Our bearded host, Leo Herbert, who was next to Sybil with the entrance door at his back, was the first to speak.

"It is very strange, but just before Hans put Sybil under, I felt that there was a draft. I got up, and shut the door, but I could still feel this coldness, right here, on me. It just never left, and feels pretty much like that this moment, though not with the intensity it had when you were hypnotizing Sybil. I had the feeling if I moved out of this spot, Sybil would talk louder."

Sybil's entranced voice was not loud on this occasion, and some of the group farther back in the room had difficulty hearing her.

"Did you have any psychic experiences in this house prior to our session tonight?" I asked Leo Herbert.

"I have heard noises from upstairs, where I sleep, and I came down here to investigate and found no one here," Herbert said, "but I had the feeling of a *presence* here. As if somebody had just been here. This was only two and a half weeks ago. The first time when I awakened, I thought that I heard footsteps down here, and I waited a long time and heard nothing, and after fifteen minutes, I went back to bed. An hour later I was awakened again, went directly down, checked the windows and door and found them all locked. Yet I felt someone had been present here."

I then turned to Mrs. Herbert, who was sitting on the comfortable couch next to Catherine.

"What about you — have you had any uncanny experiences here?"

"About a year ago, I was alone in the apartment," the slender brunette answered, "when I was sure someone was throwing pebbles against the skylight of the roof above our bedrooms. I also heard footsteps on the roof."

"Did you look to see who it was?"

"No, I was terrified."

"Did you find any pebbles on the roof?"

"No, nothing. I went up the next morning, but there was nothing on the roof. No pebbles."

I thanked Mrs. Herbert and approached the Nearys, who live below the Herberts. Mrs. Neary was quite willing to talk to me, although she had originally been a skeptic about ghosts.

"The sounds in the house are so much more varied than ever before," she volunteered. "I have heard a bell ringing, yet there is no bell. On at least six occasions lately, I have felt someone brush past me, yet nobody could be seen. I have had a sense of shadow. There are all sorts of strange noises. Primarily in the area of the wall between the living room and kitchen. Sometimes there is ticking in the wall."

I asked for quiet, and read aloud Miss Montreuil's letter to me, relating the experiences she had had at the house while a guest of previous tenants. I stressed that Sybil Leek did not know where we would be going that evening. She had no advance information, because we never discuss cases beforehand. I had directed the driver to take us to 420 West Forty-Sixth Street, carefully avoiding the use of "Clinton Court." On arrival, I had hustled her upstairs, so that she had no chance to study the house or familiarize herself with it.

And yet much of what came through Sybil Leek's entranced lips matched the earlier testimony of Ethel Johnson Meyers. Much was new, too, and could be checked without much difficulty. I felt Ethel had "sensed" a girl on the staircase, and so had Sybil.

That the stairs had been moved was unknown to both Ethel and Sybil at the time, yet both said they had been. Sybil spoke of a man hanged on the stairs, which might very well refer to Old Moor, the sailor hanged for mutiny on the Battery, but buried here in Potter's Field. Clinton Court was built above the old Potter's Field.

The girl, waiting for someone and for something to happen, was felt by both mediums. And the story of the pebbles and footsteps on the roof meshes with Mrs. Meyer's tale of a girl pushed off the roof to her death.

The officer named Walker was a new character in the ever-expanding ghostly cast of Clinton Court. Could he be traced?

Sometimes it is even difficult to trace a living officer, and tracing a dead one isn't easy. I did not expect to be completely successful, but I had hoped that at least one or two names could be traced or proved correct.

Sybil, in trance speaking with the voice and mind of Col. George Walker, had referred to a commanding officer by the name of Amos Wilson. He also said his doctor was one Dr. Warren, and that he had come to New York in 1788. We don't know, at least from the psychic end, whether he was still on active duty in 1792, when presumably his death occurred. He might have been retired and his visit to New York might not have been connected with his military career at all.

It was therefore with considerable interest that I found in Heitman's *Historical Register of Officers of the Continental Army* that a George Walker had been a Second Lieutenant, serving in that capacity to 1783, and that one Amos Wilson, First Lieutenant, had served at least in 1776; also, one John Warren, Surgeon, is recorded for the period from 1777 to 1783. These officers served with Northern regiments, while Walker claimed North Carolina as his home. However, it was not unusual for officers, or men, for that matter, to serve in regiments based in other regions of the country than their own colony. Many Southerners did indeed come north during the revolutionary and post-revolutionary period to serve with established "Yankee" regiments.

In trance, Walker claimed to have had a brother named Aaron Walker, with the rank of Captain. I found a Lt. Aaron Walker, attached to a Connecticut regiment in 1776. George Walker — the one I found listed — served in New Jersey, incidentally, which could have brought him into nearby New York.

I did not locate Walker's other brothers, nor did I come across his father or wife, but we must keep in mind that the records of the period are not complete. Certainly the claimed friendship with George Clinton fits in chronologically. The ghost also spoke several times of a place called Brice, North Carolina, and described it as being near Pike's Hill. There is a Pikes*ville*, North Carolina.

As for Brice, North Carolina — or perhaps Bryce, as the spelling was never given — this took a bit more searching. Finally, the reference librarian of the North Carolina State Library in Raleigh, Mrs. Helen Harrison, was able to supply me with some information.

The *Colonial Records*, which is a list of incorporated towns, early maps, postal guides, etc., revealed nothing about such a place. The State Department of Archives and History also checked their files without success. But in *Colonial Records*, vol. IV, page 16, there is *mention* of a sawmill being erected at Brice's Creek, Newbern, in 1735, and of Samuel Pike receiving a land grant at Newbern in 1748.

"Brice started to acquire land grants as early as 1707," Mrs. Harrison pointed out, "and it is known that Brice built a fort on his plantation and that patents were granted for land on Brice's Creek as late as 1758. It seems possible that this settlement may be the Brice to which you refer."

What about Pike's Hill and Three Hills, which the ghost said were close to each other and to Brice?

"In 1755," Mrs. Harrison stated, "there was a movement to build the capital at Tower Hill, Craven County, N.C. It interested me to find that *all three* of these places are located in Craven County, though Tower Hill may have no connection with Three Hills."

On re-hearing the tapes, I find I cannot be absolutely sure whether the ghost said Tower Hill or Three Hills. It could have been either.

So there you have it. How could Sybil Leek (or I, for that matter) know these minute details that are so obscure even a local historian had difficulty tracing them?

Not a ghost of a chance, I think.

The Teen-Agers and the Staten Island Ghost

I receive a great many letters from people between the ages of twelve and eighteen who have a serious, often very inquisitive interest in extrasensory perception. Sometimes they have a case of their own to report.

Such was the case when I first heard from Carolyn Westbo, who lived on Staten Island. It seemed that her aunt, Mrs. Carol Packer, had lived in a house on Staten Island where a poltergeist had also taken up residence. Poltergeists are ghosts who like to make noises or move objects around.

Carolyn's aunt no longer lived at the house. I asked the new owners, a family by the name of Goetz, for permission to visit.

What I liked about Carolyn Westbo, who was seventeen and very serious, was that she herself was doubtful about her experiences and wondered if they weren't all due to imagination or, as she put it, "self-delusion." But deep down she knew she was psychic, and had already accepted this knowledge.

"When were you at the house on Henderson Avenue the last time, Carolyn?" I asked.

"The last time I was at the house was in January of 1965," she answered. "My aunt was in the process of moving out, and the house was in an uproar. I stood against the wall and watched the proceedings. My left side was turned to the wall, and I was reminiscing about the wonderful times I had had on New Year's Eve, and somehow smiled to myself. All of a sudden, my *right side*, the right side of my head, felt very depressed and a feeling of great despair came over me. I felt like wringing my hands and was very distraught. It only stayed with me a few moments, but I had the distinct feeling of a woman who was very worried, and I could almost feel something or someone pressing against the right side of my head. And then I saw a mist, in the large downstairs dining room of the house."

"A mist? What sort of mist?"

"It had a shape, rather tall and thin. It did not have a face, and looked kind of ragged. *But I did see hands wringing.*"

Carolyn had told her aunt about her uncanny experience, even though she was afraid she would be laughed at. Her own family had pooh-poohed the whole thing, and Carolyn did not like to be laughed at, especially when she *knew* she had seen what she had seen. But her aunt did not laugh. She, too, had observed the misty shape when she was alone in the house, yet she had always felt great comfort with the ghost, whoever it was.

It was then that Carolyn learned about the poltergeist on Henderson Avenue. Objects were moving by themselves, her aunt admitted, such as things falling from a table and other objects that hadn't been touched. On one occasion she heard a loud crash downstairs — the house had three stories — and found a freshly baked pie upside down on the floor. She had placed it far back on the shelf in the pantry. Pots and pans around the pie had not been touched, and no trucks were passing by outside that might account for the vibration that could have caused the pie to fall. There had been nobody else in the house at the time. The aunt, Carol Packer, now lives in upstate New York. She had never accepted the idea of a ghost, and yet could not offer any explanation for the strange happenings in the house.

"Have you had other experiences of a psychic nature?" I asked the young girl.

"Nothing really great, only little things, such as knowing what my teacher would ask the next day, or what people are wearing when I talk to them on the telephone or dream about them. I see things happening and a week later or so, they do happen."

Carolyn and her aunt had looked into the history of the house. They found that three families prior to Mrs. Packer's stay in the house, a woman had dropped dead on the front porch. They never knew her name or anything else beyond this bare fact.

There the matter stood when our little expedition consisting of Sybil Leek and myself, book editor Evelyn Grippo, and CBS newscaster Lou Adler and his wife, arrived at the Victorian structure where the ghost was presumably awaiting us. Mr. Adler brought along a CBS radio car and an engineer by the name of Leon, who we almost lost on the way over the Verrazano Bridge. It was a humid Sunday evening in May of 1965. Fifteen people had assembled at the Goetzes' to celebrate some kind of anniversary, but I suspect they were very curious about our investigation as an added attraction. We could hear their voices as we mounted the steep wooden steps leading to the house from Henderson Avenue, a quiet street lined with shade trees.

While the CBS people set up their equipment, I politely put the celebrants into the front room and collected those directly concerned with the haunting around a heavy oak table in the dining room on the first floor of the sturdy old house. Carolyn Westbo, her younger sister Betsy, Mr. and Mrs. Goetz, their son and a married daughter,

Mrs. Grippo of Ace Books, the Adlers, and I formed a circle around the table. I had asked Sybil to wait in another room, where she could not possibly overhear a single word that was said in the dining room. Afterwards, skeptical reporter Lou Adler admitted that "unless she had some sort of electronic listening device by which she could listen through walls, or unless you and Sybil set this up to trick everybody — there is no alternative explanation for what occurred this evening." Needless to say, we did not use electronic devices. Sybil could not hear anything, and neither she nor I knew anything of what would happen later.

As soon as Sybil Leek was out of earshot, I started to question the witnesses among those present. Carolyn Westbo repeated her testimony given to me earlier. I then turned my attention, and my microphone, to Betsy Westbo.

Betsy had been to the house a number of times. Had she ever felt anything unusual in this house?

"One time I walked in here," the serious young girl said in response. "My mother and my cousin were in the kitchen downstairs, in the rear of the house, and I walked into the hall. It was dark, about sunset, and I suddenly felt as if someone were staring at me, just looking at me. I was sure it was my cousin, so I asked him to come out. He had played tricks on me before. But he wasn't there, and I went into the kitchen, and he had not left it at all."

"Any other experiences bordering on the uncanny?" I asked.

This 15-year-old girl was calm and not at all given to imagination, I felt, and she struck me as mature beyond her years.

"The time my aunt moved out, I was here, too. I felt as if someone were crying and I wanted to cry with them. I was just walking around then, and it felt as if someone were next to me crying and saying, 'What's going to happen to me?'"

Betsy had also had psychic experiences in her young life. Not long before in her family's house, just down the street from the haunted house her aunt used to call home, Betsy was asleep in bed around 11 P.M., when she awoke with a start.

"I heard a screech and a dog yelping, as if he had been hurt. I was sure there had been an accident, and we looked out the window, but there was nothing, no car, no dog."

"What did you do then?"

"We couldn't figure it out," Betsy answered, "but the very next evening, again at eleven o'clock, we heard the same noises — my sister was with me in the room this time. We checked again, and this time there was a dog. I had seen the entire accident happen, *exactly as it did, twenty-four hours before!*"

"Amazing," I conceded. "Then you are indeed clairvoyant."

Mrs. Mariam Goetz, a pleasant-looking, vivacious woman in her middle years, had been the lady of the house since February of 1965. She had not seen or heard anything uncanny, and she felt very happy in the house. But then there was this strange business about the silver —

"My silver spoons disappeared, one by one, and we searched and searched, and we thought someone was playing a prank. Each blamed the other, but neither Mr. Goetz, nor my son, nor my young married daughter, Irene Nelson, who lives with us, had hidden the spoons. The wedding gifts were displayed in Grandmother's room upstairs, including some pretty silver objects. One evening, after about a week of this, we discovered in each bowl — a silver spoon! Of course we thought Grandmother had been playing a trick on us, but she assured us she had not."

The rest of the spoons turned up in the drawers of the room, carefully hidden in many places. Although the grandmother was quite aged, she was in good mental condition, and the Goetzes really had no proof that she hid the spoons.

"Irene, my married daughter, had come to sleep with me several nights, because she hadn't felt very secure in her own bedroom," Mrs. Goetz added.

Mrs. Irene Nelson was a young woman with dark eyes and dark hair, not the dreamer type, but rather factually minded and to the point. She had been in the house as long as her parents, four months to the time of my investigation.

Had she noticed anything unusual?

"Yes," the young woman said. "One night I was sitting in the kitchen at the table, with two friends of mine, and as we sat there and talked, some screws were falling to the floor from the kitchen table, by themselves, one by one. My friends left. I got up to gather my things, and the table collapsed behind me. One of its legs had come off by itself. But the table was not wobbly, or any of the screws loose, just before we used it, or we would have noticed it. There was nobody else in the house who could have loosened the screws as a prank, either."

"And poor Grandmother can't be blamed for it, either," I added. The octogenarian did not get around very much any more.

"Anything else?" I asked, crisply.

"One night, about four in the morning," Mrs. Nelson said, "I woke up with a sudden start and I opened my eyes and could not close them again. Suddenly, I felt pin-prickles all over my body. I felt chilly. I felt there was someone in the room I could not see. I heard a strange sound, seemingly outside, as if someone were sweeping the sidewalk. This was in my bedroom directly above the living room. The feeling lasted about ten minutes, and I just lay there, motionless and frightened. I had several bad nights after that, but that first time was the worst."

"Have you ever felt another presence when you were alone?"

"Yes, I have. In different parts of the house."

The house, along with the building next door, was built at the turn of the century. It was Victorian in architecture and appointments. Heavy wooden beams, many small rooms on the three floors, high ceilings, and solid staircases characterized the house on Henderson Avenue.

It was time to bring Sybil Leek into the dining room and start the trance.

Had anything happened to her while she was waiting outside in the kitchen? Sybil seemed somewhat upset, a very unusual state for this usually imperturbable psychic lady.

"I was standing by the refrigerator," she reported, "and the kitchen door opened about two inches. It disturbed me, for I did not want anyone to think I was opening the door to listen. There was someone there, I felt, and I could have easily gone into trance that moment, but fought it as I never do this without you being present."

Imagine — a ghost too impatient to wait for the proper signal!

"I wanted to run outside, but restrained myself," Sybil added. "I never moved from the spot near the refrigerator. I was terrified, which I rarely am."

We sat down, and soon Sybil was in deep trance. Before long, a faint voice made itself heard through Sybil's lips.

"What is your name?" I asked.

"Anne Meredith." It came with great difficulty of breathing.

"Is this your house?"

"Yes . . . I want to get in. I live here. *I want to get in!*"

"What's wrong?"

"I . . . have . . . heart trouble . . . I can't get up the steps."

Sybil's breathing was heavy and labored.

"How long have you lived here?"

"Thirty-five."

"What year did you move in?"

"Twenty-two."

"Were you alone in this house?"

"No . . . James . . . these steps . . . James . . . son."

"What is it you want?"

"I can't stay here . . . want to get in . . . the steps . . . can't get to the door . . . *door must be opened.*"

"How old are you?"

"Fifty-two."

"Where did you go to school?"

"Derby . . . Connecticut."

"Your father's name?"

"Johannes."

"Mother's?"

"Marguerite."

"Where were you baptized?"

"Derby . . . my lips are sore . . . I bite them . . . I have pain in my heart."

I started to explain her true status to her.

"You passed out of the physical life in this house," I began. "It is no longer your house. You must go on and join your family, those who have passed on before you. Do you understand?"

She did not.

"I have to get up the stairs," she mumbled over and over again.

As I repeated the formula I usually employ to pry an unhappy ghost away from the place of emotional turmoil in the past, Sybil broke out of trance momentarily, her eyes wide open, staring in sheer terror and lack of understanding at the group. Quickly, I hypnotized her back into the trance state, and in a moment or two, the ghost was back in control of Sybil's vocal apparatus. Heavy tears now rolled down the medium's cheeks. Obviously, she was undergoing great emotional strain. Now the voice returned slowly.

"I want to come in . . . I have to come back!"

"You died on the steps of this house. You can't come back," I countered.

"Someone's there," the ghost insisted in a shaky voice. "I have to come back."

"Who is it you want to come back to?"

"James."

I assured her James was well taken care of, and she need not worry about him anymore.

"Don't leave me outside, I shall die," she said now.

"You *have* died, dear," I replied, quietly.

"Open the door, open the door," she demanded.

I took another tack. Suggesting that the door was being opened for her, I took her "by the hand" and showed her that someone else lived here now. No James. I even took her "upstairs" by suggestion. She seemed shocked.

"I don't believe you."

"This is the year 1965," I said.

"Fifty-five?"

"No, sixty-five."

There was disbelief. Then she complained that a dog kept her up, and also mentioned that her mother was living upstairs.

What was the dog's name?

"Silly dog . . . Franz." A dog named Franz was unusual even for a ghost, I thought. Still, people do like to give their pets strange names. The Goetzes had named their aged spaniel Happy, and I had never seen a more subdued dog in my life.

Why was she afraid of the dog? I asked the ghost.

"I fall over him," she complained. "My heart . . . dog is to blame."

"But this happened in 1955, you say."

"Happened *today*," she answered. To a ghost, time stands still. She insisted this was 1955. I strongly insisted it was 1965. I explained once more what had happened to her.

"Not dead," she said. "Not in the body? That's silly."

Unfortunately, very few ghosts know that they are dead. It comes as a shock when I tell them.

"I'm going upstairs and neither you nor that dog will stop me," she finally said resolutely.

I agreed to help her up the stairs.

"Lift me," she pleaded.

Mentally, we opened the door and went upstairs.

"Where is my mother?" she said, obviously realizing that her mother was not there. I explained she had died. The truth of the situation began to dawn on Anne Meredith.

I took advantage of this state of affairs to press my point and suggest her mother was awaiting her outside the house.

"May I come back sometime?" the ghost asked in a feeble voice.

"You may if you wish," I promised, "but now you must join your mother."

As the ghost faded away, Sybil returned to her own body.

She felt fine, but, of course, remembered nothing of what had come out of her mouth during trance. Just before awakening, tears once more rolled down her face.

I thought it rather remarkable that Sybil, in her trance state, had brought on a female personality who had died of a heart attack on the outside steps leading to the house. Sybil had no way of knowing that such a person actually existed and that her death had indeed taken place some years ago as described.

What about the names Anne Meredith and James?

Carolyn Westbo checked with the lady who had owned both houses and who lived in the one next door, a Miss Irving. Quite aged herself, she did not recall anyone with the name of Anne Meredith. By a strange coincidence, her own first names were Anne Adelaide. Derby, Connecticut, exists.

Checking church registers is a long and doubtful job at best. Finding a record of Anne Meredith would be wonderful, of course, but if I didn't find such a record, it didn't mean she never existed. Many tenants had come and gone in the old house atop the hill on Henderson Avenue. Perhaps Anne and Meredith were only her first and middle names.

Time will tell.

Meanwhile, it is to be profoundly hoped that the hand-wringing lady ghost of Staten Island need not climb those horrible stairs any longer, nor cope with dogs who have no respect for ghosts — especially ghosts who once owned the house.

The Phantom
Admiral

I had never heard of Goddard
College until I received a letter from Jay Lawrence, a second-semester student at Goddard College in Plainfield, Vermont. Mr. Lawrence was serious about his interest in psychic phenomena and he had some evidence to offer. He did more than ask me to speak at the college on extrasensory perception; he invited me to come and have a look at a ghost he had discovered in Whitefield, New Hampshire, about two hours' drive from Goddard.

The haunted house in Whitefield belonged to the Jacobsen family who used it as a summer home only. The younger Jacobsen, whose first name was Erlend — they're of Norwegian descent — invited us to come stay at the house, or at least have a look at it. The Goddard College boys offered to pick us up in Boston and drive us up through the scenic White Mountains to Whitefield.

We arrived at dusk, when the country tends to be peaceful and the air is almost still. The house was at the end of a narrow, winding driveway lined by tall trees, hidden away from the road. There was a wooden porch around three sides of the wooden structure, which rose up three stories.

We were welcomed by Erlend Jacobsen, his wife, Martha, and

their little boy Erlend Eric, a bright youngster who had met the ghost, too, as we were to find out.

Inside the house with its spacious downstairs dining room and kitchen, decorated in a flamboyant style by the Jacobsens, we found Mr. and Mrs. Nelson, two friends of the owners, and Jeff Broadbent, a young fellow student of Jay Lawrence.

Sybil puttered around the house, indulging her interest in antiques. I mounted my tape recorder to hear the testimony of those who had experienced anything unusual in the house. We went upstairs, where Sybil Leek could not very well hear us, and entered a small bedroom on the second floor, which, I was told, was the main center of ghostly activities, although not the only one.

The house was called "Mis 'n Top" by its original owner and builder. I lost no time in questioning Erlend Jacobsen, a tall young man of thirty on the Goddard College faculty as an instructor, about his experiences in the old house.

"When my parents decided to turn the attic into a club room where I could play with my friends," Erlend Jacobsen began, "they cut windows into the wall and threw out all the possessions of the former owner of the house they had found there. I was about seven at the time.

"Soon after, footsteps and other noises began to be heard in the attic and along the corridors and stairs leading toward it. But it was not until the summer of 1956, when I was a senior in college and had just married, that I experienced the first really important disturbance."

"1955, Erlend," the wife interrupted. Wives have a way of remembering such dates. Mr. Jacobsen blushed and corrected himself.

"1955, you're right," he said. "That summer we slept here for the first time in this room, one flight up, and almost nightly we were either awakened by noises or could not sleep, waiting for them to begin. At first we thought they were animal noises, but they were too much like footsteps and heavy objects being moved across the floor overhead, and down the hall. We were so scared we refused to move in our beds or turn on the lights."

"But you did know of the tradition that the house was haunted, did you not?" I asked.

"Yes, I grew up with it. All I knew is what I had heard from my parents. The original owner and builder of the house, an admiral named Hawley, and his wife, were both most difficult people. The admiral died in 1933. In 1935, the house was sold by his daughter, who was then living in Washington, to my parents. Anyone who happened to be trespassing on his territory would be chased off it, and I imagine he would not have liked our throwing out his sea chest and other personal possessions."

"Any other experience outside the footsteps?"

"About four years ago," Erlend Jacobsen replied, "my wife and I, and a neighbor, Shepard Vogelgesang, were sitting in the living room downstairs discussing interpretations of the Bible. I needed a dictionary at one point in the discussion and got up to fetch it from upstairs.

"I ran up to the bend here, in front of this room, and there were no lights on at the time. I opened the door to the club room and started to go up the stairs, when suddenly I walked into what I can only describe as a *warm, wet blanket,* something that touched me physically as if it had been hung from wires in the corridor. I was very upset, backed out, and went downstairs. My wife took one look at me and said, 'You're white.' 'I know,' I said. *'I think I just walked into the admiral.'"*

"I suppose he didn't enjoy your bumping into him in this fashion either," I commented. "Anything else?"

"I was alone in the house, in the club room, which is designed like a four-leaf clover — you can see into the section opposite you, but you can't see into the other two. I was lying there, looking out the window at sunset, when I heard someone breathing — rhythmically breathing in, out, in, out."

"What did you do?"

"I held my own breath, because at first I thought I might be doing it. But I was not. The breathing continued right next to me! I became terrified, being then only fifteen years of age, and ran out of the house until my parents returned."

I asked him again about the time *he touched the ghost*.

How did it feel? Did it have the touch of a human body?

"Nothing like it. It was totally dark, but it was definitely warm, and it resisted my passage."

"Has anything happened to you here recently?"

"About two and a half weeks ago, I walked into the house at dusk and I heard very faint crying for about fifteen or twenty seconds. I thought it might be a cat, but there was no cat in the house, and just as suddenly as it had started, the crying stopped. It sounded almost as if it were outside this window, here on the second floor."

"Is there any record of a tragedy attached to this house?"

"None that I know of."

"Who else has seen or heard anything uncanny here?"

"My parents used to have a Negro maid who was psychic. She had her share of experiences here all right. Her name is Sarah Wheeler and she is about seventy-five now. The admiral had a reputation for disliking colored people, and she claimed that when she was in bed here, frequently the bedposts would move as if someone were trying to throw her out of bed. The posts would move off the floor and rock the bed violently, held by unseen hands, until she got out of bed, and then they would stop. She was a Catholic and went to the church the next day to fetch some Holy Water. That quieted things down. But the first night of each season she would come without her Holy Water and that was when things were worst for her."

"Poor Sarah," I said.

"She was psychic, and she had an Indian guide," Erlend Jacobsen continued. "I did not put much stock in some of the things she told us, such as there being treasure underneath the house, put there by the old admiral. But eight or nine years ago, I had occasion to recall this. The house has no cellar but rests on stone pillars. We used to throw junk under the house, where wooden steps led down below. I was cleaning up there with a flashlight, when I saw something shiny. It was a cement block with a silver handle sticking out of it. I chipped the cement off, and found a silver bowl, with 'A.H.' engraved on it."

I turned my attention to Mrs. Jacobsen. She had three children, but still gave the impression of being a college sophomore. As a matter of fact, she was taking courses at Goddard, where her husband was an instructor.

It was ten years to the day — our visit was on June 11 — that the Jacobsens had come to this house as newlyweds.

"We spent one night here, then went on our honeymoon, and then came back and spent the rest of the summer here," Martha Jacobsen said. "The first night I was very, very frightened — hearing this walking up and down the halls, and we the only ones in the house! There was a general feeling of eerieness and a feeling that there was someone else in the house. There were footsteps in the hall outside our bedroom door. At one point before dawn, the steps went up the stairs and walked around overhead. But Erlend and I were the only ones in the house. We checked."

Imagine one's wedding night interrupted by unseen visitors — this could give a girl a trauma!

"Two weeks later we returned and stayed here alone," Mrs. Jacobsen continued, "and I heard these footsteps several times. Up and down. We've been coming here for the last ten years and I heard it again a couple of weeks ago."

"Must be unnerving," I observed.

"It is. I heard the steps overhead in the club room, and also, while I was downstairs two weeks ago, the door to the kitchen opened itself and closed itself, without anyone being visible. Then the front door did the same thing — opened and shut itself.

"Along with the footsteps I heard things being dragged upstairs, heavy objects, it seemed. But nothing was disarranged afterwards. We checked."

"Any other events of an uncanny nature?" I asked as a matter of record. Nothing would surprise me in *this* house.

"About ten years ago, when we first moved in, I also heard the heavy breathing when only my husband and I were in the house. Then there was a house guest we had, a Mrs. Anne Merriam. She had this room and her husband was sleeping down the hall in one of the single rooms. Suddenly, she saw a figure standing at the foot of her bed."

"What did she do?"

"She called out, 'Carol, is that you?' twice, but got no answer. Then, just as suddenly as it had come, the figure dissolved into thin air.

"She queried her husband about coming into her room, but he told her that he had never left his bed that night. When this happened on another night, she attempted to follow the figure, and found her husband entering through another door!"

"Has anyone else had an encounter with a ghost here?" I asked.

"Well, another house guest went up into the attic and came running down reporting that the door knob had turned in front of his very eyes before he could reach for it to open the door. The dog was with him, and steadfastly refused to cross the threshold. That was Frank Kingston and it all happened before our marriage. Then another house guest arrived very late at night, about five years ago. We had already gone to bed, and he knew he had to sleep in the attic since every other room was already taken. Instead, I found him sleeping in the living room, on the floor, in the morning. He knew nothing about the ghost. 'I'm not going back up there any more,' he vowed, and would not say anything further. I guess he must have run into the admiral."

What a surprise that must have been, I thought, especially if the admiral was all wet.

"Three years ago, my brother came here," Mrs. Jacobsen continued her report. "His name is Robert Gillman. In the morning he complained of having been awake all night. A former skeptic, he knew now that the tales of ghostly footsteps were true, for he, too, had heard them — all night long in fact."

Jeffrey Broadbent was a serious young man who accompanied Jay Lawrence to the house one fine night, to see if what they were saying about the admiral's ghost was true.

They had sleeping bags and stayed up in the attic. It was a chilly November night in 1964, and everything seemed just right for ghosts. Would they be lucky in their quest? They did not have to wait long to find out.

"As soon as we entered the room, we heard strange noises on the roof. They were indistinct and could have been animals, I thought at first. We went off to sleep until Jay woke me up hurriedly around six in the morning. I distinctly heard human footsteps on the roof. They slid down the side to a lower level and then to the ground where they could be heard walking in leaves and into the night. Nothing could be seen from the window and there was nobody up on the roof. We were the only ones in the house that night, so it surely must have been the ghost."

Jay Lawrence added one more thing to this narrative.

"When we first turned out the flashlight up in the attic, I distinctly heard a high-pitched voice — a kind of scream or whine — followed by footsteps. They were of a human foot wearing shoes, but much lighter than the normal weight of a human body would require."

Jerry Weener also had spent time at the haunted house.

"In early March of 1965, Jay and I came over and had dinner at the fireplace downstairs. We decided to sleep downstairs and both of us, almost simultaneously, had a dream that night in which we met the admiral's ghost, but unfortunately on awakening, we did not recall anything specific or what he might have said to us in our dreams. A second time when I slept in the house, nothing happened. The third time I came over with friends, I slept in the attic, and I heard footsteps. We searched the house from top to bottom, but there was no one else who could have accounted for those steps."

Erlend Eric, age eight going on nine, was perhaps the youngest witness to psychic phenomena scientifically recorded, but his testimony should not be dismissed because of his age. He had heard footsteps going up and down and back up the stairs. One night he was sleeping in the room across the hall when he heard someone trying to talk to him.

"What sort of voice was it?" I asked. Children are frequently more psychic than adults.

"It was a man's," the serious youngster replied. "He called my name, but I forgot what else he said. That was three years ago."

Miriam Nelson was a petite young woman, the wife of one of Erlend Jacobsen's friends, who had come to witness our investigation that evening. She seemed nervous and frightened and asked me to take her to another room so I could hear her story in private. We went across the hall into the room where the figure had stood at the head of the bed and I began my questioning.

"My first experience was when Erlend and I brought a Welsh Corgi up here; Erlend's parents were here, too. I was downstairs in the library; the dog was in my lap. Suddenly I felt another presence in the room, and I could not breathe anymore. The dog started to bark and insist that I follow him out of the room. I distinctly felt someone there.

"Then on a cold fall day about four years ago, I was sitting by the stove, trying to get warm, when one of the burners lifted itself up about an inch and fell down again. I looked and it moved again. It could not have moved by itself. I was terrified. I was alone in the house."

I had heard all those who had had an encounter with the ghost and it was time to get back downstairs where the Jacobsens had laid out a fine dinner — just the right thing after a hard day's drive. A little later we all went up the stairs to the top floor, where Sybil stretched out on a couch near the window. We grouped ourselves around her in the haunted attic and waited.

"I had a feeling of a *middle* room upstairs," Sybil said, "but I don't feel anything too strongly yet."

Soon Sybil was in deep trance as we awaited the coming of the admiral — or whoever the ghost would be — with bated breath. The only light in the attic room was a garish fluorescent lamp, which we shut off, and replaced with a smaller conventional lamp. It was quiet, as quiet as only a country house can be. But instead of the ghost speaking to us directly and presumably giving us hell for trespassing, it was Sybil herself, in deep trance "on the other side," reporting what she saw — things and people the ordinary eye could not perceive.

"I'm walking around," Sybil said. "There is a man lying dead in the middle room. Big nose, not too much hair in front, little beard cut short now. There is a plant near him."

"Try to get his name, Sybil," I ordered.

"I'll have to go into the room," she said.

We waited.

"He is not in here *all* the time," she reported back. "He came here to die."

"Is this his house?"

"Yes, but there is another house also. A long way off. This man had another house. Hawsley . . . Hawsley."

Almost the exact name of the admiral, I thought. Sybil could not have known that name.

"He went from one house to another, in a different country. Something Indian."

"Is he still here and what does he want?"

"To find a place to rest because . . . he does not know in which house it's in!"

"What is he looking for?"

"Little basket. Not from this country. Like a handle . . . it's shiny . . . silver . . . a present. It went to the wrong house. He gave it to the wrong house. He is very particular not to get things confused. It belongs to Mrs. Gerard at the other house. He usually stays in the little room, one flight up. With the fern. By the bed."

"But what about Mrs. Gerard? How can we send the package to her unless we get her address?" I said.

"It's very important. It's in the wrong perspective, he says," Sybil explained.

"What did he have for a profession?" I tried again.

"He says he brought things . . . seeds."

"What are his initials or first name?"

"A. J. H."

Sybil seemed to listen to someone we could not see.

"He's not troublesome," she said. "He goes when I get near to him. Wants to go to the other house."

"Where is the other house?"

"Liang . . . Street . . . Bombay."

"Does he know he is dead?"

"No."

I instructed her to tell him.

"Any family?"

"Two families . . . Bombay."

"Children?"

"Jacob . . . Martin."

It was not clear whether the ghost said Jacob or Jacobsen.

"He is shaking himself," Sybil now reported. "What upset him? He worries about names. A. J. A. name on something he is worried about. The names are wrong on a paper. He said Jacobsen is wrong. It should be Jacob Hawsley son."

Evidently the ghost did not approve the sale of his house by his executors, but wanted it to go to his son.

"Because of two houses, two families, he did not know what to do with the other."

"What does 'A' stand for in his name?"

"Aaron . . . Aaron Jacob."

"Does he have any kind of title or professional standing?"

"A-something . . . A-D-M . . . can't read . . . Administrator A-D-M . . . it's on the paper, but I can't read the paper."

Still, she did get the admiral's rank!

I promised to have the gift delivered to Mrs. Gerard, if we could find her, but he must not stay in this house any further.

"Who waters the plants, he asks," Sybil said.

I assured him the plants would be taken care of.

"But what about the other house, who waters the plants there?" the ghost wanted to know.

"How does he go there?" I asked in return.

"He sails," Sybil replied. "Takes a long time."

Again I promised to find the house in India, if I could.

"What about a date?" I asked. "How long ago did all this happen?"

"About 1867," Sybil replied.

"How old was he then?"

"Fifty-nine."

I implored the admiral not to cause any untidiness in the house by upsetting its inhabitants. The reply via Sybil was stiff.

"As a man with an administrative background, he is always tidy," Sybil reported. "But he is going now."

"He is going now," Sybil repeated, "and he's taking the ferns."

I called Sybil back to her own body, so as not to give some unwanted intruder a chance to stop in before she was back in the driver's seat, so to speak.

None the worse for her travels in limbo, Sybil sat up and smiled at us, wondering why we all stared at her so intently. She remembered absolutely nothing.

Erlend Jacobsen spoke up.

"That basket she mentioned," he said. "When my parents first bought the house, there was hanging over the dining room, on a chain, a stuffed armadillo, which had been shellacked from the outside. It had straw handles and had been turned into a *basket*. It was around the house until about five years ago, but I have no idea where it is now. For all we know, it may still be around the house somewhere."

"Better find it," I said. "That is, if you want those footsteps to cease!"

Just as we were leaving the house, the senior Jacobsens returned. Mr. Eric Jacobsen does not care for ghosts and I was told not to try to get him to talk about the subject. But his wife, Josephine, Erlend's mother, had been pushed down the stairs by the ghost — or so she claims. This is quite possible, judging by the way the admiral was behaving in his post-funeral days and nights.

Our job in Whitefield seemed finished and we continued on to Stowe, Vermont, where we had decided to stay at the famous Trapp Family Lodge. Catherine had become interested in Mrs. Trapp's books, and from *The Sound of Music*, we both thought that the lodge would provide a welcome interlude of peace during a hectic weekend of ghost hunting.

The next morning we rested up from the rigors of our investigation and found the world around us indeed peaceful and promising. The following morning we would go down to Goddard College and address students and teachers on the subject of ghosts, which would leave us with a pleasant afternoon back at Stowe, before flying back to Manhattan. But we had reckoned without the commercial spirit at the lodge. Like most overnight lodgings, they wanted us out of our rooms by eleven o'clock Sunday morning, but finally offered to let us stay until two. I declined.

After my talk at the college, we were taken to one of the girls' dormitories where uncanny happenings had taken place. The college was situated on the old Martin farm, and the manor had been turned into a most elegant girl students' residence, without losing its former Victorian grandeur. Reports of a dead butler still walking the old corridors upstairs had reached my ears. Two students, Madeleine Ehrman and Dorothy Frazier, knew of the ghost. The phenomena were mainly footsteps when no one was about. A teacher who did not believe in ghosts set foot in the manor and later revealed that the name Dawson had constantly impressed itself on her mind. Later research revealed that a butler by that name did in fact live at the manor house long ago.

Sue Zuckerman was a New York girl studying at Goddard.

"One night last semester," she said, "I was up late studying when I heard footsteps approaching my room. After a few seconds I opened my door — there was nobody there. I closed the door and resumed studying. I then heard footsteps walking away from my door. I looked again, but saw nothing.

"During this time for a period of about three weeks, my alarm clock had been shut off every night. I would set it for about seven-thirty, but when I woke up much later than that, the alarm button was always off. I began hiding my clock, locking my door — but it still happened.

"Back in 1962, I was toying with a Ouija board I had bought more in fun than as a serious instrument of communication. I had never gotten anything through it that could not have come from my own mind, but that Friday afternoon in 1962, I worked it in the presence of three other friends, and as soon as we put our hands on it, it literally started to leap around. It went very fast, giving a message one of us took down: 'I am dead . . . of drink." Are you here now in the Manor?' 'One could speak of my presence here.' There was more, but I can't remember it now.

"Afterwards, a strange wind arose and as we walked past a tree outside, it came crashing down."

I don't know about strange "wind," and Ouija boards are doubtful things at times, but the footfalls of the restless butler named Dawson must have been a most unusual extracurricular activity for the co-eds at Goddard College.

The Somerville Ghost

"**I'**m Mrs. Campano," the letter read in a large, clear handwriting, "and I've been living in this house for four months now." The woman had heard me on station WBZ, Boston, and wanted to report a haunted house.

I called her and found Mrs. Campano a reasonable, well-spoken lady in her middle years. Her elder daughter had recently married and her son was grown, and it made sense for the mother to move to a smaller house. But at the moment she was still at the haunted house on Washington Avenue in Somerville, Massachusetts.

The first impression that something strange went on in her house was when she noticed her dog's unusual behavior. The dog barked constantly and kept running up and down the stairs to the upper floor. When the daughter moved out, she took the dog with her, and Mrs. Campano's house became quiet *except for the ghost*.

There was a light in the downstairs living room of the wooden house, so she found it unnecessary to turn on any additional lights when she wanted to mount the stairs. One night in 1964, when she passed the stairway, she heard someone crying. She entered the bathroom, and when she came out she still heard the sound of someone crying as if hurt. She walked up the stairs, thinking it was one of her children having a nightmare, but when she got to the top of the stairs, the crying stopped.

She checked all the rooms upstairs, and the children were fast asleep. She went back to bed downstairs. Then, above her head, she distinctly heard the shuffling of feet, as if two people were fighting and struggling. She had a puppy, who started to act strangely just as the larger dog had done.

The experience upset Mrs. Campano no end, and she talked it over with her elder daughter, Marsha, now married. The girl was sympathetic, for she, too, had heard the crying and at one time footsteps of someone going up and down the stairs, with the crying continuing for about twenty minutes. It sounded like a woman.

They decided to do something about the noises. A group of young boys, friends of her son's, stayed overnight at the old house. They took the upstairs room where most of the disturbances centered. At first, everything was quiet. The youngest girl and some of her friends went to sleep in another room upstairs. Soon the boys heard tapping and crying, but thought the girls were trying to put over a practical joke. They jumped from their beds and raced across the hall only to find the girls fast asleep in their room.

Mrs. Campano turned to the church for relief, but the local priest refused to come. A friend supplied her with Holy Water but the relief was short lived. A week later, noises started up again.

When Marsha, the elder daughter, had the bedroom to the right upstairs, she often heard the crying and felt as though someone were touching her. But she had kept quiet about these sensations. After she had moved out, the younger daughter, who had the room now, also reported that she felt a presence in her room, and something or someone unseen touching her feet as if to rouse her!

The eighteen-year-old son also had heard the footsteps and crying and had decided to check on the source. When he had reached the hallway, the crying suddenly stopped, but the puppy, which had come with him, kept on growling. Ten minutes later the noises started up again, this time from the cellar.

One more thing Mrs. Campano found strange about the house: on the wall of the room upstairs there was a red spot that looked like blood.

I reached Jim Tuverson, of WBZ's "Contact" program, to arrange for a visit to the haunted house on Washington Avenue, Somerville.

There was a problem, though. Mrs. Campano had decided to move out on May 31, 1965, and our visit would be in June. We took it up with the landlord, Costa & Sons. This is not so easy as it sounds. How do you tell a real estate man one of his properties is haunted? You don't tell him, that's how. You do tell him you've got an interest in old New England houses and could you do a little historical research?

When we arrived at the house I realized immediately how funny the request must have sounded to Mr. Costa. The house was a ramshackle, run-down structure. Since Mrs. Campano had moved, we agreed to see her *after* the investigation and trance session.

It was a warm day for Boston when we met Jim Tuverson and Bob Kennedy of WBZ at Logan Airport. Sybil Leek had flown in directly from San Francisco — using an airplane of course — and joined us for the ride to the haunted house. She knew nothing whatever about the case, not even the location of the house. We left our cars in front of the house where a few curious people had gathered. They rarely saw two radio cars pull up in this unglamorous section of town.

Quickly we went inside the house where a lady from the real estate firm of Costa & Sons was expecting us. The house had been stripped of all its contents except the dirt, which was still around in generous quantities. The aroma was somewhat less than heavenly and it was my fondest wish to get out of there as soon as possible. It was about four in the afternoon and bright, but Sybil never lets such things bother her when we investigate a place.

We hastily borrowed a chair from the house across the street and assembled in the kitchen downstairs. Sybil took to the chair, and I began the session by asking for her impressions of this dismal house.

"As you know, I came in and walked right out again and got a drink next door — that's always a bad sign for me. I don't like this place at all, and I don't think we're in the right room. The upstairs room is the right place."

"What do you feel about the upstairs?"

"There is a strange smell in one of the rooms upstairs, not just a physical smell, but something beyond that. I always associate this smell with something quite evil and I don't think I'm in for a good time."

"What do you think has taken place in this house?" I asked.

"I think there has been some violence here," Sybil replied without hesitation, "the right hand room upstairs."

"Do you feel any presence in this house?"

"I feel a very bad *head* right now," Sybil said and touched the back of her own head as if she felt the pain herself. "My head is very bad. There is some lingering evil which pervades not only the inside of the house, but even the outside is not immune."

I then asked Sybil to relax as well as she could under these uncomfortable circumstances, and to allow whatever entity might be hovering about to communicate through her.

Outside the warm air was filled with the distant noises of a bustling city, but inside the drab, dirty house, time seemed to stand still as we tried to wedge open a doorway into another dimension.

"Things are different today," Sybil finally said. "I'm looking in at the house — but nobody can speak through me."

We should have gone upstairs to the room Sybil thought was the center of the haunting, I thought. Still, one never knows. Sometimes just being in a house, any place within the walls, is sufficient to make contact.

I instructed Sybil to remain in trance and to report back anything she could find.

"Right hand side," Sybil said in a quiet, slow voice, different from her habitual speech. "There's someone in the house . . . it's a girl."

"What do you see upstairs?"

"I see the girl on the bed. She's got long, wavy hair, she can't get up, her head is very bad."

"Is she injured?"

"Yes . . . in the back. She's dead. There's a child or a dog, a child . . . this is 1936 . . . I keep going outside the house, you see, because there's someone around . . . I can't find him."

"Can you speak to the woman on the bed?"

"She worries about the child."

I explained about her true status and where the child now was.

"She's getting angry," Sybil reported. "She does not believe you."

I told Sybil to instruct the woman how to call for her child. But the ghost was very confused. We tried to get her to follow Sybil out of the house. I kept explaining what had happened to her.

"She won't leave until she finds the child," Sybil explained and I kept thinking of the scurrying footsteps on those stairs, the crying — it all fitted in with a mother trying to find her baby!

"What is her name?" I asked.

There was silence as we waited for more evidence from Sybil's lips.

"Linda Mathews," Sybil said, clearly and distinctly.

"And the child's name?"

"Margaret."

I had never heard these names before in connection with this case, nor had anyone else in the room. Mrs. Campano had not mentioned them to me either.

I instructed Linda to call for her child and then leave the house. But she wouldn't budge.

"She's waiting for someone . . . Robert Shaw was here, she says."

"Did *he* hurt her?"

"She'll kill him, because she hates him enough. He hurt her. He hit her."

"Did he kill her?"

"She doesn't know."

"Did her husband kill her?"

"She doesn't know."

Again Sybil, on my urging, explained her situation to the ghost.

"She's coming a little closer now," Sybil reported. "I think she's Scotch. Country type. She's moving now, off the bed. I'm with her. She's very weak."

I told Sybil to withdraw as soon as the ghost was safely outside the house. Quickly I brought her out of trance.

"Quite an ordeal, somehow," Sybil said, although she did not remember anything that had come through her while in trance. I sent her and my wife on to the radio station with Bob Kennedy, while Jim Tuverson and I drove in his car to Mrs. Campano's new house, a few blocks down Washington Avenue.

The new house was much smaller and the Campanos occupied only a part of it, but it was brighter and much more cheerful than the house we had just left.

A sudden idea struck me. I walked into the Campano living room, and shot a question at Mrs. Campano —

"Have you ever heard of Linda Mathews?"

"Yes," Mrs. Campano replied with surprise. "I used to get her mail at the old house all the time, and always sent it back. She used to live in the house. In fact, she died there. But I don't know any more than that."

Here we had immediate corroboration of a name — not a common name like Jones or Smith, but a definite name not easily guessed — and information concerning this name had not been known to anybody in the haunted house while we were there!

Thus Sybil could not have gotten the name from the unconscious minds of any of us in the house, nor indeed from me, since I had only learned of the Mathews matter this minute. Jim Tuverson was visibly impressed. Here was proof of the kind that would stand up in any court of law. Sybil had really done a superb job.

I questioned Mrs. Campano about her experiences at the house. Was there anything she had not told me prior to my coming to Somerville?

"It was like a woman crying as if she had been hurt," she reiterated. "Then one night I was the last one to go to bed and everything seemed perfectly normal. In the morning, however, I discovered a series of pictures, which I have in the room between bookends, placed on the floor as if by human hands. Nobody could have done this."

I thought perhaps the unfortunate woman ghost had been trying to get her attention.

"What about your husband?" I asked. "Has he ever heard anything unusual?"

"Yes. One morning we came in around 3 A.M., and we were in the kitchen downstairs cooking, when we both heard someone coming down the stairs. He thought one of the children had smelled the food and was about to join us, but, of course, nobody appeared."

"What about you and your son hearing those footsteps coming up from the cellar?" I asked.

"It sounded like someone in heavy boots coming up the cellar steps," Mrs. Campano explained, "and then we heard the noise of someone handling pots and pans in the kitchen."

"Were they actually moved around?"

"Yes. The next morning we found the kitchen in disorder, but nobody had been in who could have done this. No burglars, either."

I began to wonder if the cellar at the Washington Avenue house did not hold the bodies of two murdered people.

"Did you check the cellar?" I asked.

"The next day," Mrs. Campano replied, "but we found nothing."

Mrs. Campano's father, Peter Cagliano, 73, is a mystic and probably psychic. He came to the house, and for a while things became quiet after that.

Evidently, Mrs. Campano also had inherited some of her family's psychic talents. Her first psychic experience took place when she was 17 years old. She then lived in a house where a murder had been committed and witnessed the noises and physical phenomena accompanying the haunting. Seven years ago, she saw the apparition of a woman known to have died, by the name of Jehasses, but no communication ensued.

"What do you know about a murder committed in the house you just left?" I finally asked her.

"The husband killed his wife and baby, and then himself," she replied, *"with an ax, up in one of the rooms."*

Exactly what Sybil had said in trance!

There was one more witness I wanted to question: Mrs. Campano's married daughter, Marsha Parmesano, who used to sleep in the haunted room upstairs.

"When I was asleep," she said, "I used to feel someone breathing over me, but when I turned around there was nobody there. At the edge of my bed I felt someone sitting there, like gettin' up and sittin' down, but there was no one there. That was the room to the right, upstairs. I felt it a couple of times."

After all, she was occupying Linda Mathews' bed — and adding discomfort to the ghost's unhappy state.

We left the Somerville ghost house with the conviction that the next tenant would have nothing to worry about. No more footsteps, no more crying. That is, unless there is something — or somebody — buried in the cellar that needs to be discovered.

But I doubt it even then. Sybil Leek managed to lead the murdered woman out of her self-imposed prison to join her child. Unless the allegedly guilt-laden husband is still outside the walls of the old house, unable to leave the place of his crimes, everything should be peaceful on Washington Avenue.

Come and Meet My Ghost!

Margaret Widdemer was a spirited lady in her sunny years, a famed author and prize winner, who had for years made her home in the New York studio building on West Sixty-seventh Street called the Hotel des Artistes. It was the sort of place that cries out for a ghost, modeled on European studios and full of eerie, half-lit corridors and nooks. The tenants are painters, writers, and teachers.

Miss Widdemer lived in a roomy duplex, with a pleasantly crammed living room downstairs, and a wooden staircase winding to the upper story, which was divided unevenly between her workroom and a small bedroom.

All her life, Margaret Widdemer, poet and novelist, had had psychic experiences of one kind or another. Pennsylvania-born, she had visions of the dead many times.

Miss Widdemer bought her apartment in the mid-1940s, from a Mrs. Gertrude F., who had since passed on. Mrs. F. had another apartment a few doors away herself; she, her husband, and a daughter were among the original shareholders of the building, built around 1910.

Elizabeth Byrd, a mutual friend, had told me of her uncanny feelings in Margaret Widdemer's apartment.

It intrigued me sufficiently to make an appointment for a visit, but I did not feel that the presence of a medium was required — the evidence was too slender. Thus I arrived at the Hotel des Artistes on a damp night in February, 1965, accompanied only by my tape recorder and immense good will toward whoever it was who was present in the place!

I asked Miss Widdemer what her unusual experiences in the apartment had been.

"There have been unexplained noises, bangings of doors and such, and my cleaning woman would say, 'I thought you were in.' She would say 'I just saw someone walk up the stairs' — but, of course, I was not in. The same thing would happen to me. I was here alone, and I thought my maid had come in, because I heard footsteps going up and down the stairs, but on checking I found she hadn't come in at all."

Present were Elizabeth Byrd, Mrs. L. (a psychic neighbor from across the hall), and Barrie Gaunt, the young English designer and actor whose own haunted apartment we had visited not long before down on Charles Street.

For the past few minutes, Barrie had been restless and I saw him wandering about the place, up and down the stairs, as if searching for something or someone. The house was strange to him, of course, and I thought he was just exploring with the natural curiosity of the artist. But he seemed perplexed, and I began to wonder if he had sensed anything out of the ordinary.

"Someone came up these stairs," he finally said, "stopped about here and turned around — hate in the eyes. It's a woman."

His left hand felt strangely stiff, he added. And he had a feeling that someone was murdered here.

Elizabeth Byrd, too, had had an unusual experience in the apartment in April.

"I was having dinner with Margaret, and at one point wanted to go to the powder room. I went up the stairs, and the minute I got to the top of the stairs, I was seized with fear. I blundered into the other rooms before I could get my bearings. I didn't want to yell for help, because Margaret walks with a cane and would have had to scramble up the stairs to help me. I couldn't get down again fast enough. I was really scared, and I don't scare easily."

I turned my attention once more to Barrie Gaunt.

"I feel a great tragedy here," he said, "especially on the staircase where the curve is. I feel an agonizing screaming. In the room directly above this, there is a complete turmoil. A very beautiful woman, I feel, also a man, and I feel there's been a death here, a death by violence. The woman is fighting for her life, but not physically. Rather, she is fighting for *her mentality*. The person who is dead in this apartment is the man."

Everybody stared at Barrie now, as it turned out that we had a medium among us, after all, even though I had not brought one.

"Go on," I said, but it was hardly necessary. Barrie was engrossed in his impressions.

"The tragedy involved both people in this apartment. I just know it." Still shaken with the eerie feelings that had beset him on the stairs, Barrie reiterated his conviction of a terrible struggle going on and the woman's agony stood vividly etched on his expressive face.

I decided it was time to break up our meeting, and thanked our hostess. A few days later, Margaret Widdemer was able to supply some of the answers to the questions raised by Barrie Gaunt.

"The F. girl, Christy, was a tall, very beautiful blonde with great blue eyes," she said. "When she was around seventeen, she suddenly went raving mad, and became so violent that she had to be removed.

There was a history of disturbance on both sides of the family, it is alleged, and her hatred directed itself, for reasons unknown, against her own mother. She was placed in an insane asylum at Middletown, New York. Her mother could not even visit her, so violent was the poor girl's reaction."

"Then the girl lived here for a while, before they removed her?" I asked.

"Evidently so," Miss Widdemer said, and explained that Mrs. her neighbor, had helped her gather this information.

Was it the father restraining his raving daughter that Barrie had sensed on the stairs? He was dead now, and no information on how he died was available.

The question now: Was the girl still living at the asylum? A few days later, that question, too, was answered. She had died some time ago, still raving mad.

Barrie Gaunt, of course, could not have known any of these facts. I took a series of photographs in the apartment, none of which showed anything unusual. Was it an etheric impression then that Barrie had sensed, a re-enactment of the emotional events of the past? Or was the ghost of the poor girl still holding on to her one-time home, struggling against the brute force that was to take her away from it forever?

Country House Ghosts

*I*n May of 1964, I received a telephone call from a lady who identified herself as Doris Armfield. She had read my book *Ghost Hunter*, and wanted to invite me to a house at Rehoboth, Massachusetts, where a poltergeist had taken up residence.

I asked her to give me a detailed account of her experiences.

"My husband and I purchased the house sometime around 1940. It was purported to be more than 200 years old. We have never heard that it was haunted or that any violent death had occurred in it, but the legend has persisted that this was the house that had a fortune buried somewhere in a stone wall, and we treated this story as an old-time tale.

"We have had many odd happenings at the house during the years, but the noises heard in the kitchen are what concern me. The original house was a regular Cape Cod consisting of four rooms downstairs and an attic upstairs. One hundred years after the original house was built, a kitchen ell was added, consisting of the kitchen, a small room off the kitchen, and a large back hall. Our current postmaster in town lived in the house at one time and he added dormers upstairs. We put a porch along the ell. There is also a small barn used as a garage. These constitute the physical plan of the house. We own about 100 acres on both sides of the street.

"Shortly after we moved in, the first event happened. My husband and I were eating supper in the kitchen when a sound like an explosion made us both bound from our chairs. We found that a glass dish in the kitchen cupboard on the top shelf had shattered. We decided that maybe a change of temperature had made the dish break and left it at that. However, this particular noise has been the only one where we found physical evidence of breakage.

"About two years after this, my husband joined the Navy in World War II and his aunt came to stay with me for a week or two. The first night as we sat down to supper in the kitchen, my dog Dusty sat beside my chair, and all of a sudden he started to growl very deeply. The hackles rose on his back, he bared his teeth, and scared me half to death, because I had never seen him do this unless he thought my husband or I was threatened. He was *staring at an empty chair* to my left, but I thought his growl meant someone was around the house. I went out and looked around, but no one was there.

"My aunt went home to her own house after a week or so and I lived alone in the house with the dog and some assorted cats. One night I was reading in bed, with the dog at my feet. I reached up to put off the bed lamp when I heard a tremendous crash and the sound of dishes banging, crashing, and shattering. I knew immediately that the dish cupboard in the kitchen had fallen loose from the wall and that it had hit the counter beneath it and just spewed all the hundreds of dishes across the floor and smashed them to smithereens. The dog and I flew into the kitchen only to find everything was intact. I took a flashlight and went all over the house from cellar to attic, knowing all the while that the only big quantity of dishes were in that kitchen cupboard.

"We decided to make a three-room apartment upstairs for a

girlfriend of ours who had lost her husband a few years before. She moved in, and the years went by, eighteen years, in fact.

"One evening at 5 P.M., she came home from work, and walked upstairs to her apartment. She had her foot on the last step when she just stood there unable to believe that horrible crashing and clattering of dishes being broken.

"Naturally, she expected to see the three-shelved kitchen cupboard torn away from the wall, figured it had hit the counter beneath it, and that every dish had fallen, breaking and rolling along the floor. She stood there in amazement when she found nothing was disturbed.

"We went home the next weekend, and as we compared noises, we found we had both had the same impression of what had happened, and the noises were identical. This happened about two years ago.

"About two months ago, a neighbor and myself were singing, and also playing the piano in the dining room, and were also tape recording our efforts. My husband was in the room behind the kitchen, and my sister was reading in the living room. At the end of a song we heard a crash of dishes or glasses and we all converged on the kitchen. I thought our Siamese cat had climbed onto a shelf on the hutch and possibly knocked off three or four plates that had then broken. Once again we all looked at each other and couldn't believe that nothing was broken. I then thought of the fact that the crash was on the tape, and we played it back and sure enough, we heard it loud and clear."

Immediately after I received Mrs. Armfield's report, I telephoned her at her weekday residence in Connecticut. The house at Rehoboth, Massachusetts, where the uncanny phenomena had taken place, was a weekend retreat.

I offered to come out to have a look at the house on my next trip to Boston.

"Everything is quiet for the moment," she replied, "but you're welcome any time."

Somehow the trip never occurred, and it was not until April, 1965, when I finally got around to reaching the Armfields again. I have no staff to help me, and cases just pile up until I can get around to them myself. This time my note was answered by Doris' husband, Richard Armfield. His wife had passed away in January of 1965. Under the circumstances, I decided not to trouble him, hoping that Mrs. Armfield herself might have discovered what or who it was who caused the uncanny noises in the Rehoboth house — from *her* side of the veil.

....

Charles Demers, who described himself as a combat veteran and unafraid of anything, lived with his family in an old house in Hampstead, New Hampshire. He bought the house in 1959. His two older girls — he had three children — slept upstairs in a finished room at the rear of the attic. Right away, they complained about noises in the attic. When he went to investigate, he himself heard the footsteps of a heavy person walking across the floor, night after night, at 10 P.M. The two children were moved downstairs, and Demers himself took the room in the attic.

"I have stared death in the eye many times, Mr. Holzer," Demers said, "and I was not afraid. I listened hard and sure enough, *it* was coming to the door of the bedroom. I gently slid out of bed and turned on the light, waiting. The ghost was just outside the door. I looked at the door knob, and *it was being turned slowly*. I did not panic, but nothing further was heard."

No footsteps going down, for instance.

....

Another New Hampshire case concerned a certain Mrs. V., who had been subject to the uncanny all her life. On more than one occasion she had seen an apparition of her own father, especially when she was in some sort of difficulty. The house she and her second husband occupied in a small town in New Hampshire was very old. There was a little door leading up to the attic. A narrow staircase ascended to the attic, and for no apparent reason, the door kept opening by itself. Someone walking about in the attic, softly, as if in stocking feet, had become an almost daily occurrence. Finally, she asked around, and found out that the house had once belonged to an old man who had been abused and put into the attic. The man finally cut his throat, and was buried in the family cemetery nearby. It was his house once, but his people apparently took it away. And now he was back in command once more.

....

Mae Ramirez was a widow in her late thirties, with three children, who lived in a small town in the Cape Cod area. I talked to her on the telephone at length and she struck me as pretty level-headed, although she seemed scared of ghostly visitations. Small wonder, with the ones she had.

There was a certain young man her father disliked very much. She stopped seeing him when she got married, but after her divorce many years later, she took up with him again.

Her father had died in 1945, and Mrs. Ramirez left Massachusetts soon after, only to return in 1954. Shortly after she had placed some flowers on her father's grave after her return to Cape Cod, she woke one night from deep sleep with the fearful feeling that she was not alone in the room. Groping for some matches she had put under the pillow, she was unable to find them. In the semi-darkness her eyes fell upon the left side of her pillow where she distinguished the outline of a man. Finally she overcame her fears, and sat up in bed. Before her stood her late father, dressed in dark clothes, looking directly at her. Without saying a word, he left slowly and quietly.

"I heard the steps," Mrs. Ramirez said, "but when he reached the stairs, he did not go down, *but through the wall.* Afterwards I went downstairs, and checked the doors, looked in closets, and there was no one there."

After she stopped seeing the young man her father had disapproved of, the ghost of her father never returned.

....

Jane Morgan had a house in Kennebunkport, Maine, that was full of ghosts. I had talked to her time and again, offering my services and those of Sybil Leek to help her get relief. But she didn't want to free her house from its ghosts. To begin with, her brother, who shared ownership in the house with the talented singer, had for years insisted that there was nothing to the story.

"You may have discussed the hauntings in my house with my sister," he said cheerily, "but I live here and I assure you there ain't none!"

I thanked Mr. Currier — Currier is Jane Morgan's real name — and forgot all about it, for, let's face it: I've got more unsolved hauntings to take care of than an army of parapsychologists could handle. But the whole controversy — was there or wasn't there a ghost at Jane Morgan's place — was brought to mind again when the *New York Daily News*, November 16, 1964, quoted the singer as saying:

"I don't want to have them exorcised. That would be cruel. They might have no other place to go . . . and besides, I'd miss these friendly spirits."

Having read *Ghost Hunter*, Miss Morgan knew perfectly well what happens to a freed ghost, and that the "place" they are helped to reach is infinitely more joyous than a musty New England mansion.

Because of an exciting séance I held with Ethel Johnson Meyers in a New York apartment, a piece appeared in the *New York World Telegram* in which columnist Norton Mockridge described the procedure we used. He was swamped with mail from people with similar problems, he says, although I never saw the letters. But he did manage to follow up his first piece with an interview with Jane Morgan in which she unburdened herself of the whole story of her ghosts.

Ned, a revolutionary soldier, had killed his girlfriend Nellie's other lover, and since that time, he and his lady-love had cavorted in the old house, kept there, presumably, by their guilt feelings. Their laughing and moaning had been heard by many. Doors opened and closed by themselves at night and spectral figures had been seen flitting from room to room. Visitors, it was alleged, had spoken of a "lady in gray" in the hall who did not return their greetings, and there was a sealed coffin in the cellar of the house.

"I had a medium at the house," Miss Morgan told me, but when she mentioned her name, I confessed I had never heard of her.

"She refused to stay at the house," Jane Morgan continued, and explained that for that reason anyone else would not be likely to succeed either. I patiently explained the rather considerable difference between a successful parapsychologist and a timid medium who runs at the first chilly sign of a *real* ghost!

All the same, Jane Morgan refused to allow us to have a go at it. Meanwhile, Norton Mockridge reported that playgoers at the nearby Kennebunkport Playhouse frequently saw a man in Colonial uniform and a woman framed in the window of the haunted house across the road. They usually took them for actors rehearsing for the next week's play.

The Curriers have, however, abandoned the house for another place not far away. The new tenants didn't complain about any ghostly visitations. But then Ned and Nellie may have needed some time to get used to their new keepers.

....

The John Jay House near Bedford Village, Westchester, New York, was a museum maintained by the county. Restored exactly as it was when one of America's founding fathers, Chief Justice John Jay, lived in it, it had the reputation of being haunted. "Was there anything to it?" I asked the curator, Lewis Rubenstein.

"According to family tradition," the curator explained, "Mrs. William Jay, wife of the second of the Jays to live permanently at Bedford, saw the ghost of her mother-in-law in one of the bedrooms. Two guests at widely spaced intervals are also reported to have seen the apparition."

Although he personally did not put stock in such stories, Mr. Rubenstein extended a cordial invitation for me to visit the house.

"We know that discovery of a ghost would be good for business," he said, "but we would prefer that people came to see the site for its real historic value rather than for its other somewhat tenuous merits."

When I finally got around to making an appointment to see the house in the company of a good medium, Mr. Rubenstein got cold feet, it seems. Retracting his invitation, he referred the decision to the trustees. Otto Koegel, board chairman, informed me curtly that I was not welcome. Maybe the ghostly mother-in-law was afraid I'd dislodge her.

The Girl Ghost on Riverside Drive

One day in January of 1965, a gentleman named H. D. Settel called me on the phone to report a ghost in his Victorian apartment on Riverside Drive in New York City. Since I also live on the Drive, it seemed the neighborly thing to do to go have a look. Mr. Settel, who was in his late twenties or early thirties, had lived in the fourth floor walk-up apartment of what was once a small townhouse for some time. He got married and his wife joined him there in October of 1964.

Since moving in, his normally cheerful wife had gone into fits of despondency for which there seemed to be no rational explanation. Spending a lot of time at home, she felt a great anxiety at times, as if something momentous were about to happen. Gradually, the sensation changed to one of dissociation, a desire to leave her physical body. Fighting this tendency, she reported the strange sensations to her husband, who was sympathetic, and suggested she stop fighting the "take-over." When she followed his advice, she found herself crying for no apparent reason.

This was followed by most unusual behavior on her part. In the middle of the night, she sat up in bed and started to talk in a most irritated fashion. Unfortunately, neither of the Settels remembered the substance of her outbreak.

About mid-January, Mrs. Settel was on the threshold of sleep when she heard a curious tapping sound on the dresser. Quickly she turned on the light and the tapping stopped, but she had the fleeting impression that there was someone else in the apartment, and the strange, floating sensation came back.

Her husband also had an unusual experience. He awoke one night toward five in the morning, and asked his wife whether she had screamed. She assured him that she hadn't. Trying to get hold of himself, Settel explained that he had just heard a young girl scream. He had seen a girl dressed in a maid's uniform standing in the doorway of the two-room apartment, looking into the bedroom, and holding a large white dog on a leash. *Her look was one of pure evil.*

Somehow he had the impression that her name was Eudrice, and he felt himself compelled to write down the words "Eudrice was a girl of young looks." Neither phrasing nor handwriting was his own. The Settels had never heard of anyone named Eudrice, so they called the public library and were told that it was a Colombian form of the Greek name Eurydice.

I asked whether either of them had had psychic experiences before coming to the house on Riverside Drive.

On their honeymoon, Mr. Settel saw a very old lady during the night, and described the vision in great detail to his wife the next morning. From the details of appearance, dress, brooch, room, and chair in which he saw her sitting, Mrs. Settel realized that her husband had seen her long-dead grandmother, with whom she had lived as a child. Her husband had never seen a picture of her. Mr. Settel was in the textile business, and Mrs. Settel used to be a radio and television broadcaster.

I offered to visit the house, and did so the last week of February,

1965. The apartment on the fourth floor was done in modern style, and the Settels had made the most of the small area. There was a curious closet that suggested there had once been a door near the entrance to the bedroom. In the old days, the servants' quarters usually were located on the top floors, and this apartment undoubtedly was once just that.

I questioned Mr. Settel about the ghostly maid. Was there any light in the room at the time?

"Well, the sun was just coming up, and I could distinguish her outline quite clearly. She was a girl in her middle twenties, I'd say," he replied. "She was completely solid and real, not transparent or wavering. She had very long black hair, extremely white skin. I was terrified, stared at her for about thirty seconds, just lying there. Next thing, she was gone. We turned on the light, but, of course, there was nobody but us two in the apartment."

"What else have you observed here?" I asked.

"There was, and is, an oppressive heaviness in the atmosphere of this place, and a constant feeling of a presence other than our own," Mr. Settel replied. "Usually at night, between 9 and 3 A.M."

I turned again to Mrs. Settel.

"I almost committed suicide here once, something I would not normally think of," she confided. "Sometimes I seem to be almost possessed — I have the feeling if I allowed myself to leave my physical body, I would not be able to return."

The house had been built in 1897, and bought in 1910 from the builder by a Mrs. Gillen from Detroit. Before the house was built, the area had just been woods. From the time Mrs. Gillen bought the house, around 1910, Wall Streeters and such notables as Thomas Dewey had lived in the house. It had been a townhouse, subdivided by Mrs. Gillen into plush apartments.

There were five floors. The Settels had the fourth floor. A man named Alleyn had come to the house in 1925. From Panama, and married to a West Indian woman, he died in the house in 1956 — he dropped dead, it seems, on the second floor.

For twenty years, the Settel apartment had been owned by a retired Army colonel named Villaflora and his wife. He was from Panama and she was Polish.

The Settels were able to get a lot of information about the building from one of the older tenants, a Mrs. Morgan. The superintendent's wife had committed suicide in the apartment downstairs.

The information thus obtained left a gap between 1897 when the house was built, and 1910 when it was sold to Mrs. Gillen. Thirteen years of mystery. Many interesting tenants coming and going!

I encouraged the Settels to use a Ouija board to see if their combined psychic acumen would obtain anything evidential.

"Did you get anything worthwhile?" I asked. Ouija boards often aren't reliable. It all depends on what checks out, of course.

"Yes indeed," Mr. Settel replied. "We got so much we stopped — in a hurry. The communicator identified herself as Eudrice Fish. She claimed to have come from Germany, and to have died in 1957 by suicide. Much of it was garbled."

I took some photographs of the apartment, but none of them showed anything unusual. I had decided there was nothing more I could do in this case, when I received an urgent call from Mrs. Settel.

"Three nights after your visit, Mr. Holzer," she said, "I was lying in bed. It was about 4 A.M., and I was not asleep, having just turned out the lights. Suddenly, the bedsheet was pulled down from around my neck to below my chest. I did not move or attempt to awaken my husband, who was asleep beside me. A few minutes later, the corner of the pillow beneath my head moved *as though it were being tugged*, and I began to sense a presence. The air seemed heavy and expectant, and briefly I felt myself floating again. To my surprise, nothing further occurred, and I fell asleep in about five minutes after that.

"The night before — it was a Thursday; you were here on Tuesday — I went into the bathroom to find the water running in the sink. Neither of us had left it on. We are quite neat about such things. The bathroom also houses our cat, who seems to behave strangely at times lately. Last Christmas we went out and left the bathroom door open for her to go to her sandbox. On our return it was firmly closed — something the cat could not have done!"

I promised to come again, and this time bring Sybil Leek with me to see if contact with the ghost could be made.

Before I came, Mrs. Settel had a strange dream. She saw a male figure, and received the impression that she was very fond of this unknown man. She believed in him, but he was really quite evil. He seemed to be trying to talk her into something, and sway her. She was wondering if the ghost was trying to tell her something about her own life.

When I brought Sybil Leek to the apartment, a change took place in Sybil's face almost as soon as she set foot inside the door. The Victorian staircase and appointments outside had pleased my antique-loving friend, but when she had settled herself into the easy chair in the larger of the two rooms, she said immediately:

"It's not very pleasant here. I feel a person here who died very badly. It's a man. Something affecting his back. There is a younger person with him. They are dark, curly head, the man has a beard. European, Polish. About 1900. Something was lost here."

We adjourned to the bedroom, and Sybil went into trance. Soon she would be deeply "under."

A heavy male voice announced his presence.

"Oscar."

"Do you live here?" I asked.

"Yes."

"Your second name."

"Tratt. Oscar Tratt."

"Where are you from?"

"Efla. Near Cracow."

"What is your profession?"

"Make shoes. Out of wood. Wood shoes."

"Who lives here with you?"

"Mella. Woman. My *Gnaedige Frau*. My wife."

"Whom do you pay rent to?"

"Flynn. Sammy Flynn."

"What year is this?"

"1902."

"How old are you now?"

"Sixty-three."

"Are you well?"

"No. I'm waiting for Ernst to come back."

"Who is Ernst?"

"Mella's boy."

"Your son?"

"Who knows?"

"Why do you want him to come back?"

"Burn him."

"Why?"

"Took too much money from me." The ghost's voice rose in anger. "She let him take it!"

It wasn't clear whether he worked for Mella or whether she was his wife or both.

I continued the questioning.

"Did you get hurt here?"

"Yes, I broke my back. Ernst . . . his door by the steps, on this floor." Now the ghost broke into tears.

"I'm lost . . . find Ernst."

"Is there anyone else here? A woman perhaps?"

You could imagine the ghost shrugging, if ghosts can shrug.

"Common girl. They come and go. Looking for Ernst. Bad. Takes anybody's money . . . my back . . . bad boy."

"What is his family name?"

"Tratt . . . my son."

Schratt or Tratt — I couldn't be quite sure.

The son was about 35 and single, the ghost claimed. He belonged to the Jewish faith, and was somehow connected with a synagogue on Ninety-sixth Street. He also went to school on Ninety-sixth Street.

The ghostly voice began to falter and Oscar complained that he could not remember some things, and that his back hurt him.

"Did you go to the hospital?" I asked.

"No. Stayed here till they come for me."

"Why are you troubled?"

"Lost a lot of money here. Want to make some more shoes."

I began to send him away, gently, but firmly. After he had slipped out of Sybil's body, the medium's own personality reappeared, called back by me.

I asked Sybil, still entranced, to look around and report to me what she observed.

"There are lots of people at the top of the stairs . . . two men and two women. A man is falling down the stairs . . . and a little girl is crying."

"How old is the little girl?"

"Very pretty, like a little foreign girl. She's a servant. Perhaps 20 years old. She has a gray dress with a high neck. She's very unhappy because of what happened. She was upstairs, then she came down and hid in the cupboard . . . here. She was frightened of the young man that he might hurt her."

"Did she know him well?"

"Very well. He liked her."

"Was there anything between her and the young man?"

"Yes. She liked him, but she liked the old people, too. She used to listen to them quarrel."

"What were her duties in this house?"

"She had to look after a lot of gentlemen who lived in this house, but not really after these two here."

"What was her name?"

"Irene . . . Eurine . . . Erundite . . . Eireene." Sybil's voice expressed uncertainty.

"Why is she here?"

"No place to go."

"How did she die?"

"Very sick in her throat . . . died here. She never told anyone about the old man. My throat's bad . . ." Sybil was taking on the "passing symptoms" of the spectral maid.

"How long ago did she die?"

"1912."

Suddenly another person was speaking to us. A very agitated voice calling for "Mella!" Evidently, the servant girl had taken over. The throat seemed to hurt her still. Eventually she calmed down.

"What is your name?" I asked.

"Erundite." It could have been Erundice, or something like that.

"Where were you born?"

"Here . . . 27 London Place . . . down by the river."

I asked her to repeat her name. It now sounded like "Irene Dyke."

Her mother's name, she said, was Martha, and her father's Mostin Dyke. Or it could have been Austin Dyke. The voice was faint.

She did not know where her father came from. Only that it was far away where there were ships.

"What was your work here?"

"Servant. Laundry maid."

"Were there any pets in the house?"

"There was always something to fall over. Parrot. Ten cats."

"Any dogs in the house?"

"Oh, there was this big old monster . . . he was gray."

"Did you take him out?"

"He followed me."

"What sort of clothes did you wear when you served here?"

"Gray dress, and black apron . . . there is no water in the house, you know. Got to get some across the road. Dog fell into the river."

"What year is this?"

"1907-1908."

"Did you have an affair with Ernst?"

"I'm not going to say."

"Did you see him hurt his father?"

"Yes."

"What did you do after that?"

"I came in with Mella and I waited in the cupboard. I cried. Somebody came, that's why I stayed in the cupboard."

"Was Oscar gone then?"

"Think so. Never saw him again."

Everybody, it would seem, accused Ernst. He came back, and she saw him, but then her throat started to bother her.

"Why are you still here?"

"Mella said wait here in the cupboard."

She thought it was 1913. I coaxed her to leave the closet, and to forget about her bad throat.

"1913 I had my worst bad throat. It was very cold by the river. I went back to the cupboard."

"You're free now," I said. "You may leave this cupboard . . . this house . . . and join your loved ones."

Gradually, the tense body of the medium slackened as the servant girl left.

Soon, Sybil Leek was back to her old self.

"I feel fine," she said, and looked around. She remembered nothing of Oscar or the servant girl.

And there it is. How do you trace the name of a servant girl, even so unusual a name as Eurydice, or Irene Dyke, or whatever it was, in a rooming house in 1913? You can't. Telephones were still rare then, and the directories were far from complete.

Needless to say, Sybil knew nothing whatever about "Eurydice" or that a servant girl had been seen here by Mr. Settel. I had kept all that to myself.

Apparently, Oscar has made his peace with Ernst, and the pale young servant girl is forever out of the cupboard. The spot where Mr. Settel had seen her apparition was indeed where an old cupboard had been made into a walk-in closet. As for the big dog, why, there may be a place for him, too, on the other side. At any rate, the Settels have heard, seen, and felt nothing since Sybil's visit.

A Final Word

As always, I welcome *written* inquiries from people who have had uncanny experiences of one kind or another, be it a ghost encounter, a haunting, or some other extrasensory perception, if accompanied by a self-addressed, stamped envelope.

Those in trouble, I will try to help. Those wishing to contribute to the better understanding of this subject by telling their story, I will thank. But I will not supply mediums for personal reasons.

Parapsychology needs the help of all good people just as surely as our Yankee Ghosts, just as other ghosts that I shall tell about in future books, need a helping hand.

It's the spirit that counts.

Hans Holzer

also by Hans Holzer

Ghosts and Hauntings
Gothic Ghosts
Haunted Hollywood
Ghost Hunter
Ghosts I've Met
The Phantoms of Dixie
The Lively Ghosts of Ireland
Westghosts
The Ghosts That Walked in
  Washington
The Spirits of '76
Hans Holzer's Haunted Houses
The Ghost Hunter's Strangest Cases
Some of My Best Friends Are Ghosts
The Great British Ghost Hunt
Best True Ghost Stories
In Search of Ghosts
European Ghosts
Where the Ghosts Are

Life After Death,
Reincarnation, and ESP
Beyond This Life
Born Again
Patterns of Destiny
ESP and You
The Truth About ESP
The Handbook of Parapsychology
Predictions: Fact or Fallacy?
The Prophets Speak
Psychic Investigator
The Psychic World of Bishop Pike
Possessed
The Directory of the Occult
The Powers of the New Age
Elvis Speaks From the Beyond
Psychic Photography
The Psychic World of Plants
Life Beyond Life: The Evidence for
  Reincarnation

Healing, Dreams,
Personality Expansion
Beyond Medicine
The Human Dynamo
The Psychic Side of Dreams
The Power of Hypnosis
Charismatics
How to Cope with Problems
Speed Thinking
The Vegetarian Way of Life
Astrology — What It Can Do For You
The Aquarian Age
Psycho-Ecstacy

Other Non-Fiction
The Truth About Witchcraft
The New Pagans
The Witchcraft Report
Window to the Past
Star in the East
The Ufonauts: New Facts on Extra-
  terrestrial Landings
Word Play
The Habsburg Curse
Murder in Amityville

Fiction/Novels
The Alchemist
Heather, Confession of a Witch
The Clairvoyant
The Entry
The Amityville Curse
The Zodiac Affairs
Circle of Love
The Red Chindvit Conspiracy
The Alchemy Deception
The Unicorn
The Secret of Amityville